SCHOOL LIBRARY MEDIA SERIES
Edited by Diane de Cordova Biesel

COLOR AND SHAPE BOOKS
FOR ALL AGES

by
Cathie Hilterbran Cooper

School Library Media Series, No. 18

The Scarecrow Press, Inc.
Lanham, Maryland, & London
2000

SCARECROW PRESS, INC.

Published in the United States of America
by Scarecrow Press, Inc.
4720 Boston Way, Lanham, Maryland 20706
http://www.scarecrowpress.com

4 Pleydell Gardens, Folkestone
Kent CT20 2DN, England

British Library Cataloguing in Publication Information Available

Library of Congress Cataloging-in-Publication Data

Cooper, Cathie Hilterbran, 1953–
    Color and shape books for all ages / Cathie Hilterbran Cooper.
      p. cm. — (School library media series; no. 18)
    Includes bibliographical references and index.
    ISBN 0-8108-3542-8 (alk. paper)
    1. Color—Study and teaching (Elementary)—Activity programs—United States.
2. Geometry—Study and teaching (Elementary)—Activity programs—United States.
3. Color—Juvenile literature—Bibliography. 4. Geometry—Juvenile literature—Bibliography. I. Title II. Series.

  QC496 .C66 2000
  535.6′071′073—dc21
                                                         99-053134

♾ ™ The paper used in this publication meets the minimum requirements of
American National Standard for Information Sciences—Permanence of
Paper for Printed Library Materials, ANSI/NISO Z39.48-1992.
Manufactured in the United States of America.

CONTENTS

SERIES EDITOR'S FOREWORD

The School Library Media Series is directed to the school library media specialist, particularly the building-level librarian. The series examines the multifaceted role of the librarian as educator, collection developer, curriculum developer, and information specialist. It includes concise, practical books on topical and current subjects related to programs and services.

In a format she has made uniquely her own, Cooper has produced the third in a series of guides to early concept books. Like *ABC Books and Activities* and *Counting Your Way through 1-2-3 Books and Activities,* this title is a scholarly, thoughtful, and well-written analysis of the material.

Color and Shape Books for All Ages points out that the development of more complicated concept books has made them useful with older students. It clearly defines book formats, such as board, chunky, chubby, toy, mechanical, and pop-up. The author has selected and annotated 526 color and shape books that will be useful to librarians, teachers, and caregivers.

Diane de Cordova Biesel
Series Editor

1

INTRODUCTION

Language skills and curiosity about the complex world are vital elements in a child's road to a lifetime of learning. Developing the ability to name, sort, and categorize such basic concepts as letters, numbers, colors, shapes, and sizes is an important step toward literacy. A concept is defined as an "idea of a class of objects, or a relation, normally expressed by a word" (Beard 1969) or "a generalized idea of a class of objects; an abstract notion" (*Webster's* 1970, 293). Children are exposed to concepts from the beginning of their lives, but merely learning a word, number, or letter does not mean a child truly understands the concept behind it. Concept books are one means of helping children grasp abstract concepts like color, shape, time, distance, size, mass, and other subjects through concrete examples. Some concepts, such as "red, green, and blue" or "square, triangle, and circle" can be shown in concrete form, whereas other concepts, like love and death, are more abstract and difficult to explain in a book. It is much easier to show a red triangle in a picture then it is to show the love of a parent and child. Concept books ask a child to find a certain shape, decide which is bigger, or choose the blue object. They are designed to help a reader understand the meaning of difficult words and to grasp elusive elements of their environment. Of course, although concept books do certainly play a vital role in teaching concepts, it is important to remember that nothing can substitute for "real-life" or hands-on learning. Through repeated experiences, explanations, and questions, along with exposure to visual stimulation such as concept books, young children are able to grasp abstract concepts and to come to grips with what is not always easily understood.

Concept books are a child's first informational books. They provide facts about the real world and are designed to help children see the relationship between objects, view an idea from more than one aspect, look at similarities and differences, and grasp the dimensions of an abstract idea. While concept books are traditionally viewed as useful with toddlers and preschoolers, the influx of books with lavish, intricate illustrations, interactive participation, and detailed information has expanded the audience for concept books to elementary, middle, and even older students. Concept books for older children usually begin with the familiar and move to the less familiar, from the simple to the complex. Many times a concept book does not have a plot but instead relies on descriptions, repetition, and comparisons of objects to convey an idea. At other times, a book presents a simple story with multiple examples to develop a concept and present a more complex look at the topic. Many titles that are particularly useful with older students include intricate illustrations and complex plots, and they involve the use of critical thinking skills.

While concept books cover all types of topics, this book is concerned with the concepts of color and shape. Colors define the world around us and are such an integral part of the way we see and identify objects that they are often taken for granted. In fact, colors are so important that we often label objects by their colors: orange, kiwi, celery, rose, olive, and lilac. Because children are attracted to them from an early age, colors are an easy concept to build on. The ability to discern one color from another is a simple skill, easily mastered by the very young. However, the abilities to name a color and its varying shades and hues, to distinguish between primary and secondary colors, and to see how color affects responses, moods, and attitudes take time and work.

Beginning concept books, such as *What Color?* by Anthea Sieveking or *My First Look at*

Colors (Dorling Kindersley), are excellent titles to use with toddlers and preschoolers to learn the names of colors and to associate colors with everyday objects. Primary colors and how they are mixed to form more colors is the topic of *Mouse Paint,* by Ellen Stoll Walsh. This amusing tale of three mice frolicking with paint can be used with young children and elementary students as a entertaining way to learn about a scientific topic.

Color can affect moods, elicit feelings and responses about an object or place, influence a reader's perception of a character, or create depth, contrast, and value in a picture. All of these are topics that can be introduced to toddlers and preschoolers but that can be explored in depth with older children using concept books, picture books, and more advanced informational books.

Shapes are defined as the way things look, as discerned by their outline or outer form. Shapes can be simple and easily identified, such as circles, squares, or triangles, more complex, such as spheres, cubes, and pentagons, or even abstract,

such as some modern paintings. As with colors, identification of simple shapes begins early in a child's life. Such skills as identifying shapes and describing how they connect with real-life objects can be introduced with simple concept books such as *My Very First Book of Shapes* by Eric Carle or *Color Fun* (Snapshot Book). Other titles like *Shapes* by Ivan Bulloch or a series like *The World of Shapes* by Sally Morgan can reinforce and build on the concepts of simple shapes to more complex ones. In any case, recognizing shapes helps a child build a background for the study of geometry or other mathematical disciplines. "Looking at and asking questions about shapes lead to such geometric topics as triangles, tessellations, point of a plane and conservation of space" (May, L. March 1994: 26). Recognizing and identifying shapes in illustrations and in real-life situations are also useful for delving into the emotional aspects of this element. Artists use shapes to create certain moods or feelings, to control the eye movement, and to focus on a piece of work.

CRITERIA FOR SELECTING COLOR AND SHAPE BOOKS

The criteria for evaluating and selecting concept books about colors and shapes are the same as those for any informational resource. Consider basically five areas when selecting a title: (1) accuracy and authenticity, (2) content and perspective, (3) style, (4) organization, and (5) illustration and format. In terms of accuracy and authenticity, the information or concept must be presented in a clear, unconfusing manner. The information should be accurate and up-to-date and should clearly distinguish between fact and fiction. The book should provide one or more examples of the concepts. The book's content and perspective need to be within the comprehension and interest range of the intended audience. A concept book that is clearly beyond the developmental scope of the reader loses its value. If it is a board book for a toddler, then the content should be simple, but if the intended audience is a middle school student, then the content can be much more difficult and abstract. The style of the language or text should be interesting, clear, and appropriate for the intended user. A concept book must

be organized in a simple, straightforward manner, moving from the simple to the complex. Basic colors and shapes should be introduced and thoroughly discussed before moving on to more complex topics. Then, depending on the purpose of the book, more advanced material, such as hues and shades of colors or intricate geometric shapes, can be introduced. Books intended for older audiences should include information that is clearly structured, with easy-to-use reference guides, such as glossaries or notes. For the young reader, the illustrations and format are of vital importance. The younger the reader, the simpler the illustrations. If the intent of the book is to introduce primary colors, then the illustrations should focus on these three colors and not have extraneous details that detract from the primary purpose of the pictures. Tana Hoban's *Red, Blue, Yellow Shoe* is an excellent example of a board book for young readers designed to introduce colors. Each page features one color along with the name of the color and a familiar object. *Red, Blue, Yellow Shoe* meets all the criteria for an informational book. It has appropriate content for its intended audience, with accurate information and simple and clean illustrations that fit the needs of the young reader.

VALUE OF COLOR AND SHAPE BOOKS

Concept books (such as color and shape books) stimulate discussions about the concepts' role in the world. Because colors and shapes are all around us, they make a perfect teaching tool, especially for the very young.

Beginning concept books are essential for young children. They help develop children's vocabularies, sharpen their perceptions and understanding about the world, and link real objects to abstract concepts. The language and rhythm of the words and sounds help children experiment with language, while the simple plots and characters help children acquire a story sense that is critical in developing reading skills. Concept books help children identify and classify characteristics of an object. They provide a bridge to fun and learning by stimulating creativity, raising curiosity, and delighting the senses.

USES OF COLOR AND SHAPE BOOKS

In the past, color and shape books have been perceived as useful only with preschoolers and early primary students. However, the recent explosion of creative, imaginative titles in both concept books and picture books makes them useful with all age levels, even adults. Intricately detailed illustrations, complex puzzles and games, sophisticated themes, and interactive participation all are factors that have resulted in such universal concept books.

On the simplest level, concept books can be useful to familiarize readers with basic colors and shapes. On a more complex level, the rhyme and rhythm in many simple concept books can be used to help children understand how words are made up of individual sound parts. The ability to distinguish the sounds of each part of an entire word is a fundamental skill for reading and writing.

Color and shape books as well as all kinds of concept books are useful, but they are not substitutes for actual experiences. They are best used to enhance and reinforce an idea, not as the sole source of information about a topic. A simple board book may have illustrations of "red" or "square," but unless a child can relate that color or shape to common objects found in the everyday world, the concepts have no real meaning. After the child reads the book and discusses the color red or the square shape and how and where it can be found in his or her world, the concepts take on a new concrete meaning.

At the primary and middle grades, and even for older students, color and shape books can be used for such purposes as:

- to identify primary and secondary colors and geometric shapes
- to comprehend shades and tints, light and value, and contrast
- to know where colors and shapes occur in the environment
- to reinforce the connection between objects and concepts
- to provide information about people, places, and things
- to develop visual literacy
- to stimulate vocabulary development
- to entertain and to instruct at the same time

Concept books are suitable resources for junior high and high school students as models for writing, science, and art. Older students can use the ideas and designs found in board books and early concept books as the basis for their own creations. They can select color or shape themes, design layouts, illustrations, and typestyles to create early concept or board books for young children. Color references are plentiful, both in titles about colors and in books where the character is associated with a color, such as Clifford or Harold and his trusty crayon. Such old favorites like "Little Boy Blue," "The Little Red Hen," and even "Baa, Baa, Black Sheep" can serve as models for writing color-related stories for primary students. *The Silly Story of Goldie Locks and the Three Squares* by Grace Maccarone is an excellent example of using a traditional folktale as a way to introduce basic geometric shapes. By studying how authors adapt stories to fit a particular need, students can set about creating their own concept books.

Concept books are also useful with older students for the study of the dynamics of colors or the properties of shapes. Students move beyond the stage of simple recognition and identification of colors and shapes into a world where colors and shapes take on real value. Older children learn about complementary colors then move on to discussions about responses, moods, and attitudes that are reflected in colors and shapes. In-depth research into the properties of colors and shapes might include mixing colors, how colors play with and against one another, perceptions about colors and shapes, geometric variations, and even the color and/or shape composition of objects.

After an in-depth look at colors and shapes, older children will begin to look at art and illustrations with a discerning viewpoint. Instead of just seeing a color or shape, they may analyze responses to colors, the role of shapes in setting the mood of the work of art, or how another color or shape might create an entirely different look and response to a painting, a photograph, or another work of art.

In addition to reading stories and informational books about colors and shapes, readers of all ages need to become involved in activities using shapes and colors. In this book, ideas and activities for the various subject areas follow the discussion of related books at the end of each chapter, along with a list of additional resources in the bibliography. *1-2-3 Shapes* and *1-2-3 Colors* (Warren Publishing House) are two very good books filled with dozens of activities to use with young students. Experiments that explore the properties of colors can be found in several titles, including *Over the Rainbow: The Science of Color and Light,* by Barbara Taylor, and *The Science of Color,* by Neil Ardley. Detailed projects involving shapes can be found in *The Amazing Book of Shapes: Explore Math through Shapes and Patterns,* by Lydia Sharman.

Traditionally, concept books have been used only with preschoolers and early primary age children, but that premise does not hold true anymore. The explosion of books with lavish detailed illustrations, clever paper designs, and interactive participation have expanded the use to all age levels. Simple identification of a color or shape is no longer limited to toddlers, but instead can lead to intricate discussions on the properties and dynamics of colors and shapes. The use of concept books is limited only by the imagination and creativity of the reader.

2

FOR STARTERS (BOOKS FOR THE VERY YOUNG)

Research has shown that a child who is exposed to words and sounds at an early age will have a head start on developing the skills that are necessary for reading and language development. Children begin to learn from the moment they open their eyes, and the learning process is continuous from that point on. Scientists tells us that 50 percent of a child's intelligence is developed by age four and another 30 percent by age eight (Butler 1980). Research has shown that young children are responsive and stimulated by language and language-related activities (DeSalvo 1993), supporting the relationship between early language and reading activities and lifelong readers. One of the best ways to expose infants and toddlers to words, concepts, and sounds is by reading and discussing books. Board books and movable books are ideal reading materials for the very young on their journey toward literacy.

BOARD BOOKS

During the past twenty-five years, board books for the very young have evolved from the mediocre cardboard supermarket variety to high-quality board books and imaginative, creative movable books designed not only to teach concepts but also to entertain and amuse the reader. Until the mid-1970s, board books included a catalog of familiar objects or a retelling of familiar fairy tales, all of which were illustrated with less-than-quality pictures. Then, in 1979, Rosemary Wells introduced her famous "Max" books, followed by Helen Oxenbury's bald everyday "babies," and ushered in the era of quality board books. Board books today include adaptations of best-sellers like *The Very Hungry Caterpillar* (Eric Carle), *The Rainbow Fish* (Marcus Pfister), and *Eating the Alphabet* (Lois Ehlert), popular characters like Little Critter, Barney, and Spot, and beautifully illustrated concept books such as William Wegman's *Triangle Square Circle* and Anne Geddes's *Colors*.

The term "board book" refers to a small book with sturdy pages and simple illustrations, for infants and young children. Typically, board books have durable pages, made from sturdy tear-resistant materials, which are easy to manipulate. The cover and pages usually have a glossy, wipe-clean finish and rounded corners instead of the traditional square ones, thus preventing some accidents. The baby "first" board books usually are cloth, vinyl, or nontoxic cardboard materials that are not harmful to infants who tend to pull, tug, and chew any object within reach. Illustrations show familiar everyday objects in bright colors. Toddler board books typically have six to twelve cardboard pages and range in size from four inches to about twelve inches square. The text and illustrations are often more complicated than those of baby board books. "Chunky" or "chubby" are a third type of board book for babies and toddlers. They are about three inches square and often have even thicker cardboard covers or padded laminated covers. Picture books are often reproduced in the "chunky" book size. Picture books are traditionally bigger, include more complex plots and characters, and use the same type of paper and binding that is found in adult books.

Because they are tailored to the very young, board books typically follow one of three patterns: a wordless sequence of pictures or photographs; a concept-oriented pattern introducing simple shapes, colors, sizes, or some other concepts; or a very simple story line. Board books that introduce shapes and colors tend to follow one of the latter two patterns. There are several board book series that follow a set pattern in each title that focuses on one concept. The My Little Color Library series (Dorling Kindersley) is six titles each featuring one color (i.e., blue, red, yellow, green, purple, or orange). This engaging series features items that are sometimes, usually, or almost always the featured color. Photographs of real objects decorate the pages with each object clearly labeled, helping children identify new words and the objects they are seeing. The My Little Color Library books are some of the few children's books on color that show different shades. Another series from the National Geographic Society features one color (blue, red yellow, green, purple, or orange) in each of its six small board books. However, the National Geographic series has no text and focuses only on nature scenes to introduce colors. *Blue* takes place underwater, where a crab, shell, and fish have fun, while in *Yellow,* the bright morning sun rises over a yellow flower, a bee, and a cat. Each double-page spread is a simple scene drawn from nature. Silver Burdett's Images is not a traditional board book series; it is best used with the preschool set. Each of the four books in this 1996 series concentrates on images of one color. Large, full-color photographs and clear, oversized text bring to life all sorts of familiar objects. For example, in *Green,* by Karen Bryant-Mole, grass, caterpillars, frogs, leaves, green beans, and green peppers are images children can easily identify.

Each book in the Playshapes series (by Arnold Shapiro) is in the featured shape and shows familiar things found in that shape. For example, when a child opens *Circles,* it forms a large circle. The illustrations in *Circles* show such round items as a ball, the moon, and a pizza. The text is simple identification of objects. Mavis Smith also has a series of board books that feature one shape in each book. Die-cuts of the shapes appear throughout the book to reveal things on the upcoming pages as well as being a part of a familiar object on the page. In *Squares,* the die-cut square shows that squares can be found as crack-

ers, blocks, boxes, ice cubes, and even pockets. *Crescents* shows how crescents are all around us in bananas, puppy tails, and even smiles. Both of these board book series are useful to reinforce shapes in the world around us.

Color Fun and *Shapes Galore* are part of an early concept series from Snapshot. Young readers can choose one of the tabs that runs down the side of the book and discover what the symbol on the tab means. In *Color Fun* each of the five tabs is the tip of a color pencil. Choose a tab, and the page opens to photographs of familiar objects found in a specific color. For example, choose the orange pencil, and the page opens to show carrots, a pumpkin, a fish, an orange, and even a crab. *Shapes Galore* uses the same format except that five colorful shapes are on the tabs. Choose the tab with the oval, and the page opens to reveal photographs of an egg slice, a balloon, a grape, and an oval soap among other things. Squares, circles, rectangles, and triangles are other shapes covered in this book. The text is very simple, with the concept in large black bold print and the everyday objects identified in smaller print next to the photograph. The reader can learn about shapes and new words at the same time.

Two other sets of books use tabs to help the reader select pages. In *Choosing Colors* and *Seeing Shapes,* sturdy tabs run down the right side of the book making it easy for the reader to choose a color tab or one with a shape. On the left side of the double-page spread are photographs of four objects found in the color or shape, while the facing page shows a baby or toddler playing with familiar objects. The text is simple with the name of the color or shape and the objects. On the back of each book is a guide for adults telling ways to use the book with children. McClanahan Book Company's Learn-a-Round series includes a book on colors and one on shapes. With this series, the rounded tabs run across the top of the book and down the right side and are directly connected to the rhyming text. The reader locates the object shown on the tab somewhere in the picture on the page. Both of these books make for a fun game to play with the very young child as it reinforces his or her knowledge of simple colors and shapes.

Food is a popular topic for introducing colors and shapes to the young reader. *Red Strawberry* by John Clementson, *Garden Colors* (Western Publishing), and *Color Crunch!* by Charles Reasoner are three board books that focus on colorful foods. *Red Strawberry* is the simplest of the three—suitable for babies. It introduces only five colors through simple text and plain, cut-paper pictures: red strawberry, yellow lemon, orange carrot, green apple, and purple plum. *Garden Colors* is a small board book that tells the story of Farmer Rabbit and his garden. Short rhyming lines tell the reader about the colors that Farmer Rabbit sees, while a die-cut window tantalizes the reader with a glimpse of the next page. Blueberries, orange pumpkins, and yellow corn are only some of what Farmer Rabbit harvests for a bountiful picnic under a rainbow on the last page. *Color Crunch!* also serves up the colors of the rainbow to curious readers with large appetites. Yellow bananas, purple plum pie, black bean tostadas, and pink bubble gum are among the taste treats that appear in this yummy celebration of colors. Vivid, eye-appealing illustrations accompany the rhyming text. *Color Crunch!* is part of the "Bite" board book series, with three large bites that go from cover to cover as if someone got hungry while reading. Reasoner has included primary colors, such as red, blue, and yellow, along with shades of colors, such as peach, aqua, and lavender.

In addition to these three titles, food is also central to *Time to Eat: A Shake-n-Move Book* by Dawn Bentley and *Cookie Shapes* and *Ice Cream Colors* by John Fosberg. Bentley uses familiar foods to entice young readers to learn about colors. By shaking the book, youngsters can look at different shapes of foods and colors. A green bean and a yellow banana are only two of the savory treats that are revealed behind a special window. John Fosberg offers a delectable look at colors and shapes in two recently released titles for preschoolers. In *Cookie Shapes,* young children are treated to shapes revealed in all sorts of delicious cookies: squares, circles, ovals, and more. To accompany the shapes of cookies, Fosberg tackles colors in *Ice Cream Colors.* While looking at the various hues and flavors of mouthwatering ice cream, beginning readers also learn about colors. Chocolate, pistachio, and even bubble gum are a few of the colorful ice cream treats in the scrumptious book. After reading this delicious and colorful collection of books, readers will be ready to head to the nearest refrigerator.

Familiar characters such as Little Critter and Spot from picture books and Big Bird, Barney, and Mickey from television and movies appear in many board and "toy" books. Because they are already familiar to young readers, these characters can be useful in introducing early concepts such as colors and shapes. Most of these titles present a familiar storybook character who concentrates on introducing the concept in the context of his or her original setting. Mercer Mayer's *Little Critter Shapes* and *Little Critter Colors* are excellent examples of the chunky board book genre. The text in both titles is limited to one word identification of the shape or color on the page. Little Critter and his friends (spider, mouse, and grasshopper) frolic through the pages playing with familiar things in the featured color or shape. Despite their small size, the detailed illustrations are chock-full of all kinds of brightly colored objects. To introduce blue, Little Critter explores underwater, where he sees a blue fish, boat, and starfish. Other colors are introduced as Little Critter picks carrots, plays in his sandbox, builds a snowman, and even looks at the stars.

Other concept board books with familiar book characters include Eric Hill's "Spot" series and Beatrix Potter's *Benjamin Bunny's Colors* and *Learn with Jemima Puddle-Duck: A Book of Shapes.* Spot frolics through the pages showing off colors and shapes in his world in two separate titles by Eric Hill. In *Benjamin Bunny's Colors,* Benjamin joins other Potter characters as he tells all about colors. Jemima Puddle-Duck is looking for a new house with just the right shapes in *Learn with Jemima Puddle-Duck.* The house must have just the right rectangle door, square window, and triangle roof so that she can hatch her brand new oval egg. Both books have a simple story line, making them an appropriate introduction to both concepts and characters from the Beatrix Potter's tales.

Use of characters from cartoons, television, and movies is one way to capture the readers' interest as the book introduces basic concepts. They are already familiar with the character and are interested in what the character has to say. Kermit, Big Bird, Barney, Tiny Toons, and even the Disney characters have their own books about colors and shapes. In *Baby Bop Discovers Shapes,* by Stephen White, the green baby dinosaur looks for shapes all around her. Die-cut shapes on the cardboard pages help even the youngest child find the shape on the page. Rather than focusing on the popular TV character, Baby Bop serves simply as a vehicle to emphasize shapes and how they look. Barney uses his paint set to introduce colors in Mary Ann Dudko's

Barney's Color Surprise. Rhyming text and a vibrant array of familiar objects for each color are used on the pages as Barney paints. Mickey, Donald, and the rest of the Disney gang appear in *Disney's Pop-Up Book of Shapes* and *Disney's Pop-Up Book of Colors.* Both books feature simple stories and pop-up objects throughout the books to introduce shapes and colors. For example, in the shape book, Mickey performs magic tricks that use different shapes. Big Bird and the *Sesame Street* gang are featured in several color and shape books, but two titles are of special interest to the board book group. *Baby Kermit's Color Book,* by Ellen Weiss, features the baby Muppet characters as they encounter thirteen familiar colors. Big Bird plays a guessing game with the reader in Golden Books' *Big Bird's Color Game.* A series of four to seven familiar objects are found on one page with the facing page showing Big Bird. He asks the reader to guess what object he is thinking about and gives some clues about the object. The answer is revealed on the next page.

Anne Geddes, William Wegman, and Tana Hoban are three very successful authors who have created not only color and shape books but also other board books of outstanding quality. Geddes is well known for her photo essays of babies and toddlers. In *Colors* she has outdone herself with both backgrounds and costumes. All the children in the photographs are dressed in the featured color. For example, for the color green, two babies sit on cabbage leaves and wear leaves on their heads; for red, she uses a bare baby wearing only a red hat; whereas for orange, the children perch in a pumpkin patch. Geddes's photographs are unusual, colorful, and very effective in their simplicity. William Wegman uses his famous Wegman dogs (Fay and family) as the subject for the photographs in *Triangle, Square, Circle.* The Wegman dogs are almost human in these colorful scenes featuring shapes of all sorts. The left page shows a closeup of a dog balancing a colorful shape, and the facing page shows the shape in a familiar scene, such as the dogs crowded in a semicircle tent. From sailing on a boat to being sheriff, the Wegman dogs are sure to capture the imagination and attention of any young child.

Tana Hoban is well known for her photographic essays of familiar objects in unusual ways. She has three entries in the board book field on color. *Red, Blue, Yellow Shoe* is a collection of photographs of common objects in basic colors. Hoban includes a large dot under each object as well as name identification of the color. The photographs include a blue mitten, a black kitten, and a green leaf. The other two titles, *Black on White* and *White on Black,* concentrate on the contrasting colors of black and white. Outlines of familiar objects are shown against a background of black or white depending on the book. *Black on White* features black silhouettes, such as a butterfly, leaf, and a pail against a background of white. *White on Black* uses white silhouettes, such as a sailboat, buttons, and a banana, against a black background. Once again, Hoban has conveyed a basic concept in a simple but effective manner.

MOVABLE BOOKS

In addition to the durable board book genre for the very young is a whole new category of exciting titles known as "movable, toy, or mechanical" books. Movable books come in a wide variety of formats, including pop-ups, pull-tab, lift-the-flap, die-cuts, fold-out, and any number of creative feats of paper engineering. While simple movable books have been around for years, the trend toward more intricate interactive books escalated in the 1980s. With each publishing season, the books become more and more creative with new ways of looking at old topics and even more unusual artistic designs. Although traditionally, movable books have been used with the very young, they are suitable and recommended for all ages, including adults. Intricate illustrations, complex paper engineering, and creative designs make movable books irresistible to any age group.

David A. Carter and his clever bugs have two titles that deal with colors. In *More Bugs in Boxes,* some very strange but colorful creatures inhabit the pages. Hidden inside the box on each page are special color bugs. The reader tries to answer the question about "What kind of bug?" by opening the box to see what pops out. The last page in the book holds a surprise when a box of rainbow paintbrush bugs pops up. When the reader opens the notepad to find out the bugs' names, she or he must first name the colors of the bugs. *More Bugs in Boxes* is a book to read over and over again for sheer pleasure. In *Colors,* Carter uses a simplified version of colorful bugs to introduce six basic colors. Baby bugs pop-up from the pages to introduce red, yellow, blue, green, orange, and purple. Even the youngest reader will enjoy the surprise of these unusual bugs who seem to pop up everywhere.

Colors, which is illustrated by Roma Bishop, is a small pop-up book similar to David A. Carter's. It focuses on several objects on each page in the featured color with as a simple little object that pops up from the page as it is turned. For example, the green page features a pop-up dragon with a green pea, leaf, and boot in the background. *Colors,* published by Price Stern Sloan, also uses two pop-up objects to show off colors. The double pop-ups are connected to one another in some way. For the color red, a clown appears at the bottom of the page and a balloon at the top; for green, a frog leaps off the top of the page and a lily pad opens up at the bottom. Both of these small books will appeal to the very young.

DK Publishing is well known for its informational book series, which combine beautiful photography with a wealth of facts, such as Eyewitness and Eyewitness Juniors. Its trademark is stark white backgrounds with photographs of real objects and brief, easily understandable text on each page. *Fundamentals,* by Harriet Ziefert and published by DK, is a series aimed at three levels—baby, toddler, and preschool—with bath, cloth, and board books that reinforce concepts and language. The books are encased in a clear vinyl bag for easy storage and carrying. A heavy cardboard sheet with Velcro-backed play pieces in shapes or colors comes with each book. The reader matches the play pieces to the appropriate spot in the book, practicing both matching skills and eye–hand coordination. The objects are simple, colorful, and easily recognizable, and best of all, the books are durable for little ones.

Running Press's Fit-a-Shape series also involves interactive participation with the young reader. Attached to the last page of these small board books is a clear box containing five plastic play pieces. The reader matches the play piece with the corresponding image cut in the cardboard page. All play pieces are familiar objects and are durable for small fingers. *Colors* includes a banana, carrot, flower, apple, and leaf for the reader to match with the correct color. *Shapes* includes a beach ball, cracker, starfish, slice of cake, and an oval balloon. The simple text includes a question-and-answer format, making both titles appealing to toddlers.

In yet another unusual format, *My First Book of Shapes and Colors* uses twelve plastic pieces for the reader to manipulate and match with the shapes and colors in the book. The oblong board book calls for simple identification of four basic shapes and five colors. The text consists of the name of the shape and/or color along with a one-word identification of the objects found on the page. The plastic pieces include three of each of the four basic shapes (circle, square, rectangle, and triangle), which the reader sorts, stacks, and matches. While the book contains ordinary illustrations and simple text, the combination of manipulative shapes and the text provides an excellent lesson for children in the abstract concept of shapes.

Pulling tabs to reveal a surprise or answer a question is a popular device in "toy" books. In DK Publishing's *Secret Shapes* and *Close-Up Colors,* the reader pulls a tab to reveal another picture. As the tab is pulled, the slots in the square on the page change slowly, forming another object. The square in the center of each page contains a shape or a color. When the tab is pulled, a familiar object is revealed, such as a yellow lemon, a blue butterfly, a triangular kite, or a cylindrical can of soup. The idea of using changing pictures is unique and an interesting approach to introducing concepts, but DK's pages are not particularly durable and tend to tear easily. Alan Snow offers push–pull handles in *What Color Is It? What Shape Is It?* He uses simple concepts to create a participation book about concepts. It shows familiar scenes, such as a farm or lake, throughout the book. The shape or color appears at the top of the page, and the reader must find something on the page to match. For example, on one the page, the reader must find the red hens. By pulling the handle, the hens and the answer are revealed. *Colors* and *Shapes,* by Mavis Smith, uses a turning wheel instead of tabs. By turning the wheel, the reader must find the answer to the question on the page. There are two choices shown on the wheel as the reader manipulates it.

Distinctive formats and creative paper engineering are becoming more and more prominent in the field of "toy or movable" books. Edmon J. Rodman has created a rather unusual trio of small books that come packaged together in shrink-wrap plastic and look like small cereal boxes. The *Snack Pack Books* resemble the familiar cereal boxes of Cheerios, Trix, and Chex, but the titles are *Triangles, Circles,* and *Play Squares.* The outside cover of each box includes a variety of puns and wordplay based on common phrases used in advertising and tied into the featured shape. For example, *Triangles* claims to be "3 Times the Fun!" and "made with the goodness of corners." It includes "100% of daily angles." *Circles* are "best around" and "when cut in half, provide an excellent source of semicircles." *Play Squares* claims to have "no curves added" and "provide an excellent source of cubes." Inside each of the three boxes is a small book about the shape, including pop-up objects on the pages and questions for the reader. Shapes are presented on the pages through easily read text and familiar objects. Rodman's *Snack Pack Books* trio is an interesting addition to the "movable" book category.

Music and sound effects appear more often in interactive books. Two examples in the early concept genre include *The Funny Color Band* and *Puppy's Colors.* Part of the Golden Sound Book Story Book series, *The Funny Color Band* offers six whimsical sound effects. In *The Funny Color Band,* when the reader encounters a symbol in the text, he presses the matching symbol on the sound box. In *Puppy Colors,* a cute little puppy explores the world and discovers all kinds of colorful things. The color photographs are uncluttered, and include familiar objects, such as a pumpkin, frog, and black cat. The reader must match the color dot on the page to the one on the sound box in order to hear the text question repeated along with a sound made by the colorful object. Both of these titles are a departure from the pull, tug, and pop-up variety of participation books.

The final category of movable books is the lift-the-flap variety. *Funny Shoes* by Ron and Atie Van der Meer has a surprise gift at the end of the story. All kinds of crazy, colorful shoes are found on the pages. The reader lifts the shoe to find out what crazy creatures are wearing the shoe. On the back of the shoe is a rhythmic sentence describing the type of shoe and the crazy critter wearing it. A family of frogs wears purple elf shoes, a rabbit dons brown hip boots, and a stylish spider prefers black bow-tie shoes. On the last page appears a pair of racy red slippers with real showlaces for the reader. The shoes unfold, so the child can put them on. *Funny Shoes* introduces not only basic colors, but also shades of color. Small color boxes at the top of each page show the color and how it looks in light and dark shades.

Fuzzy Yellow Ducklings, by Matthew Van Fleet, combines lift-the-flap with tactile fun for children of all ages. Colors, shapes, and animals are the focus of this very easy-to-read concept book. Every page is a surprise when a textured shape turns into a colorful animal. Each die-cut shape is filled with some kind of material for the reader to touch, including fur and sandpaper. On the left are two words describing the object, while the right side identifies the shape. Lift the flap to finish the description of the colorful creature. For example, "fuzzy yellow" is on the left, and the right page shows a circle filled with soft yellow fur. Open the flap and reveal a family of ducklings with feathers flying everywhere. The last page folds out into four panels covered on the back and front with all the story's colorful creatures.

Board books and movable books have truly come of age. Format and content know no bounds, and the genre has grown so much that only the skeptic would consider the field less than vital to a child's cognitive development. Board books and movable books are widely reviewed and judged by the same criteria as traditional literature. Board books are usually limited to a specific age level, generally regarded as preschool material. On the other hand, "toy or movable" books are very popular with preschoolers, yet they are virtually ageless in their use. The *Snack Pack Books* trio is a good example of pop-up books that are ageless. The puns and wordplay on the boxes might be better understood by middle school students than by preschoolers. The humor is definitely beyond the understanding of a three-year-old, but he or she would find appeal in the idea of a box of shapes. Many movable books serve as examples of remarkable book formats that older students might imitate while creating their own early concept titles.

BIBLIOGRAPHY

Colors

Albee, Sarah. *Allegra's Colors*. Illustrated by Peter Panas. New York: Little Simon, 1996. ISBN 0-689-80844-5.
Allegra and her friend, Mr. Cook, create delicious, colorful treats while on an exploration of the rainbow.

Albee, Sarah. *Budgie's Book of Colors*. Illustrated by Laurence Vant and Juliet Newmarch. New York: Little Simon, 1996. ISBN 0-689-80917-4.
Budgie the little helicopter zooms around the world finding all sorts of colorful views.

Allen, Jonathan. *Purple Sock, Pink Sock*. New York: Tambourine Books, 1992. ISBN 0-688-11782-1.
Tabby the cat gets dressed in a colorful array of clothing.

Arnold, Tedd, ill. *Colors*. New York: Little Simon, 1985. ISBN 0-671-77825-0.
Nursery rhymes with color words are used to introduce colors.

Barnes-Murphy, Rowan. *Colors*. Nashville, Tennessee: Ideals Publishing Corporation, 1992. ISBN 0-8249-8530-3.
Zany cats discuss what color to paint a mouse.

Bencraft, Gina. *A Week of Colours*. Illustrated by Ray Mutimer. London: Michael O'Mara Books, Limited, 1995. ISBN 1-85479-771-9.
Every day is a special day for color at the bears' school.

Bentley, Dawn. *Time to Eat! A Shake-n-Move Book about Colors*. Illustrated by Susan Tom. New York: Little Simon, 1997. ISBN 0-689-81408-9.
All sorts of tasteful treats are revealed in a special window when the reader shakes this unusual book.

Bertrand, Cecile. *Noni Sees*. New York: Lothrop, Lee, Shepard, 1993. ISBN 0-307-15685-0.
Baby Noni discovers colors in the world around her.

Big Bird's Color Game. Illustrated by Tom Cooke. New York: CTW/Golden Books, 1989, 1990. ISBN 0-307-12254-9.
Big Bird invites the reader to try and guess what object he is thinking of as he introduces colors.

Blue. Washington, D.C.: National Geographic Society, 1990.
Photographs of a colorful undersea world introduce the color blue in this small board book.

Bogdanowicz, Basia. *Yellow Hat, Red Hat*. Brookfield, Connecticut: The Millbrook Press, 1997. ISBN 0-7613-0435-5.
In this lift-the-flap book, the reader can help Bear find the right hat in the right color for him.

Boynton, Sandra. *Blue Hat, Green Hat*. New York: Little Simon, 1984. ISBN 0-671-49320-5.
All the animals show off their clothes, but a small turkey can't get his clothes on right.

Bryant-Mole, Karen. *Blue*. Parsippany, New Jersey: Silver Burdett Press, 1996. ISBN 0-382-39590-5.
Colorful photographs and simple oversized text bring to life blue socks, buttons, shirts, cars, and more.

Bryant-Mole, Karen. *Green*. Parsippany, New Jersey: Silver Burdett Press, 1996. ISBN 0-382-39589-1.
Green grass, frogs, leaves, and peppers are only a few of the colorful objects illustrated in the vivid colorful photographs.

Bryant-Mole, Karen. *Red*. Parsippany, New Jersey: Silver Burdett Press, 1996. ISBN 0-382-39586-7.
Vibrant photographs and clear text are used to introduce such red items as strawberries, apples, tomatoes, bricks, mittens, caps, and toy cars.

Bryant-Mole, Karen. *Yellow*. Parsippany, New Jersey: Silver Burdett Press, 1996. ISBN 0-382-39583-2.
Beautiful color photographs reveal yellow sunflowers, lemons, bananas, grapefruit, sandy beaches, and a bright summer sun.

Carle, Eric. *My Very First Book of Color*. New York: HarperCollins, 1985. ISBN 0-694-00011-6.
Match the colors and objects in this spiral-bound book.

Carter, David A. *Colors*. New York: Little Simon, 1993. ISBN 0-671-86875-6.
Six colorful baby bugs pop up from the pages of this beginning reader.

Carter, David A. *More Bugs in Boxes*. New York: Simon and Schuster, 1990. ISBN 0-67-16957-70.
Learning colors is fun when all kinds of strange bugs pop out of boxes.

Chardiet, Bernice. *Monkey Pop-Ups: A Book of Colors*. Illustrated by Dana Regan. New York: Scholastic, Inc., 1996. ISBN 0-590-54315-6.
As Monkey shops for a birthday gift for his friend Turtle, he can't decide which colorful toy to buy.

Choosing Colors. Designed by Barbara Sullivan; photographs by Geoff Dann. New York: Dutton, 1994. ISBN 0-525-45475-6.
Brilliant photographs of babies playing with colorful objects fill the pages.

Clementson, John. *Red Strawberry*. San Diego, California: Harcourt Brace & Co., 1995. ISBN 0-15-200314-2.
A strawberry, lemon, carrot, apple, and plum help introduce colors.

Close-Up Colors: A Changing Picture Book. New York: Dorling Kindersley, 1995. ISBN 1-56458-959-5.
Pull a tab and the colored square dissolves into a picture.

Color Fun. New York: Snapshot, 1995. ISBN 0-7894-0230-0.
Choose a tab, and discover color all around us with favorite toys, animals, and other familiar objects.

Colors. Los Angeles, California: Price Stern Sloan, 1993. ISBN 0-8431-3624-3.
Colorful double pop-ups amuse preschoolers as they learn about colors.

Colors. San Rafael, California: Cedco Publishing Company, 1997. ISBN 0-7683-2008-9.
Full-color photographs of animals are used to introduce colors.

Colors. Illustrated by Roma Bishop. New York: Little Simon, 1992. ISBN 0-671-79120-6.
Simple little pop-ups introduce colors.

Colors. Philadelphia, Pennsylvania: Running Press, 1996. ISBN 1-56138-707-X.
Readers match plastic play pieces with the correct color.

Conteh-Morgan, Jane. *Colors*. New York: Grosset & Dunlap, 1993. ISBN 0-448-40522-9.
This tall board book introduces colors using familiar objects.

Cowley, Stewart. *Yellow Fish, Blue Fish*. Illustrated by Caroline Jayne Church. Wilton, Connecticut: Joshua Morris Books, 1994. ISBN 0-89577-597-2.
As a little girl watches through a tiny window, a parade of colorful fish swim by.

Crosbie, Michael J., and Steve Rosenthal. *Architecture Colors*. New York: John Wiley & Sons, Inc., 1993. ISBN 0-471-14359-6.
Photographs of architectural elements to introduce colors.

Disney Babies Name the Color. Racine, Wisconsin: Western Publishing Company, 1987. ISBN 0-307-06045-4.
As the Disney babies play with their toys, they discover all sorts of colors.

Disney's My Book of Colors. Racine, Wisconsin: Western Publishing Company, 1995. ISBN 0-307-12517-3.
Mickey, Donald, and their friends introduce colors as they play and work.

Disney's Pop-Up Book of Colors. Los Angeles, California: Disney Press, 1991. ISBN 1-56282-020-6.
Mickey, Donald, and the gang explore the world of colors.

Dudko, Mary Ann. *Barney's Color Surprise*. Illus-trated by Margie Larsen; photographs by Dennis Full. Allen, Texas: Barney Publications, 1993. ISBN 1-57064-007-6.
Barney uses his paint set to color everyday objects.

Faulkner, Keith. *Good Night Tom: A Tiny Tom Book of Colors*. Illustrated by Jonathan Lambert. New York: Cartwheel Books, 1993. ISBN 0-590-46947-9.
Tom the cat looks for a red toothbrush among other colorful items.

Fosberg, John. *Ice Cream Colors*. New York: Little Simon, 1997. ISBN 0-689-81287-6.
Bubble gum, chocolate, and pistachio are only a few of the colorful flavors of ice cream introduced in this book.

The Funny Color Band. Racine, Wisconsin: Western Publishing Co., 1993. ISBN 0-307-74052-8.
Six sound effects and surprise songs accompany a fun-filled look at the wonderful world of colors.

Garden Colors. Illustrated by Megan Halsey. Racine, Wisconsin: Western Publishing Co., 1993. ISBN 0-307-16702-X.
Farmer Rabbit gathers the rainbow feast that grows in his garden.

Geddes, Anne. *Colors*. San Rafael, California: Cedco Publishing Co., 1995. ISBN 1-55912-013-4.
Babies and toddlers in unusual dress and settings introduce colors.

Giffard, Hannah. *Red Bus*. New York: Tambourine Books, 1993. ISBN 0-688-12443-7.
Modes of transportation introduce colors.

Green. Washington, D.C.: National Geographic Society, 1990.
A small frog and his green pond friends introduce the color green.

Greenway, Shirley. *Color Me Bright*. Halesite, New York: Whispering Coyote Press, 1992. ISBN 1-879085-53-4.
Photographs of animals and simple text are used to introduce colors.

Herbst, Judith. *Festival of Color*. Illustrations by Fabienne Boisnard. New York: Barron's Educational Series, Inc., 1991, 1995. ISBN 0-8120-6473-9.
Charming verses are used to connect colors with familiar objects.

Hewetson, Sarah. *Learn Colors*. Avenel, New Jersey: Derrydale Books, 1994. ISBN 0-517-14007-1.
Rhyming text and amusing illustrations reinforce color recognition.

Hill, Eric. *Spot Looks at Colors*. New York: G. P. Putnam's Sons, 1986. ISBN 0-399-21349-X.
As Spot plays, he finds many colorful objects.

Hoban, Tana. *Black on White*. New York: Greenwillow Books, 1993. ISBN 0-688-11918-2.
Black illustrations against a white background show such objects as a butterfly, pail, and leaf.

Hoban, Tana. *Red, Blue, Yellow Shoe*. New York: Greenwillow Books, 1986. ISBN 0-688-06563-5.
Photographs of common objects introduce colors.

Hoban, Tana. *White on Black*. New York: Greenwillow Books, 1993. ISBN 0-688-11919-0.
White illustrations against a black background show such objects as a sailboat, buttons, and a banana.

Holloway, Zena. *Colors (Water Babies)*. New York: Cartwheel Books, 1999. ISBN 0-439-04774-9.
Photographs of babies swimming are used to introduce colors.

Inkpen, Mick. *Kipper's Book of Colors*. New York: Red Wagon Books, 1999. ISBN 0-15-202297-X.
Kipper the puppy helps young children learn about colors in this entertaining board book.

John Speir's Roping Colors. Racine, Wisconsin: Western Publishing Co., 1996. ISBN 0-307-17681-9.
As the string stretches across the pages, children learn all about a rainbow of colors.

Joseph's Coat of Colors. New York: Random House, 1995. ISBN 0-679-87521-2.
Joseph tells about his coat and its colors.

Kvasnosky, Laura McGee. *Pink, Red, Blue, What Are You?* New York: Dutton, 1994. ISBN 0-525-45233-8.
Simple rhyming text and a parade of animals show off colors.

Landa, Norbert. *Rabbit and Chicken Play with Colors*. Illustrated by Hanne Turk. New York: Tambourine Books, 1992. ISBN 0-688-09969-6.
When Rabbit asks Chick to paint Easter eggs, they try to decide which colors are best.

Learn-a-Round Colors. Illustrated by Sue Cony. New York: McClanahan Book Company, Inc., 1991. ISBN 1-56293-148-2.
Rhyming verse and brightly colored illustrations introduce colors.

Lee, Kate, and Caroline Repchuk. *Snappy Little Colors*. Illustrated by Derek Matthews. Connecticut: Millbrook Press, 1999. ISBN 0-7613-0442-8.
This pop-up book of playful rhymes introduces a merry menagerie of colorful animals.

Leslie, Tamara. *Freddy the Frog: A Story about Colors*. Illustrated by Barb Lincoln. Alpharetta, Georgia: Kids II, Inc., 1994.
Freddy the frog searches for a big, black fly for lunch.

The Little Engine That Could Colors. New York: Platt and Munk, 1995. ISBN 0-844-40264-5.
A happy clown and a little engine take the reader on a ride through colors.

Longergan, Elaine. *The Sea's Many Colors*. Illustrated by Paul Lopez. Bridgeport, Connecticut: Third Story Books, 1994. ISBN 1-884506-01-1.
Baby Shamu introduces the colors of the ocean.

McCue, Dick. *Kitty's Colors*. Illustrated by Lisa McCue. New York: Little Simon, 1983. ISBN 0-671-45489-7.
Floating in the blue sky and riding in the yellow school bus are only two of the colorful adventures that Kitty has with her crayons.

McKee, David. *Elmer's Colors*. New York: Lothrop, Lee & Shepard, 1994. ISBN 0-688-13762-8.
Elmer, a patchwork elephant, shows off his colors.

McMillan, Naomi. *Baby's Colors*. Illustrated by Keaf Holliday. Racine, Wisconsin: Western Publishing Co., Inc., 1995. ISBN 0-307-12873-3.
A little girl plays with her colorful toys all day long.

Martin, Janet. *Ten Little Babies Play*. Photographs by Michael Watson. New York: St. Martins Press, 1986. ISBN 0-312-7415-1.
One by one, ten little babies introduce favorite colorful things.

Mayer, Mercer. *Little Critter Colors*. New York: Random House, 1992. ISBN 0-679-87358-9.
Little Critter explores the colors of the rainbow as he plays in the sand, swims underwater, builds a snowman, and more.

Miller, Margaret. *I Love Colors*. New York: Little Simon, 1999. ISBN 0-689-82356-8.
Color photographs of babies and their favorite things are used to introduce colors.

Murphy, Chuck. *Color Surprises: A Pop-Up Book*. New York: Little Simon, 1997. ISBN 0-689-81504-2.
An array of colorful objects are displayed in this pop-up book.

My Colors: Let's Learn about Colors. New York: Little Simon, 1995. ISBN 0-671-89829-9.
Turn the tabs to reveal familiar things in all the colors of the rainbow.

My Little Blue Book. New York: Dorling Kindersley, 1993. ISBN 1-56458-317-1.
Crayons, sandals, jeans, and blueberries are some of the blue things shown in this simple photo book.

My Little Brown Book. New York: Dorling Kindersley, 1993. ISBN 1-56458-318-X.
From cookies and gingerbread to pinecones and bears, the reader sees what is brown.

My Little Green Book. New York: Dorling Kindersley, 1993. ISBN 1-56458-316-3.
Objects that are sometimes, usually, or almost always green are featured in this board book.

My Little Orange Book. New York: Dorling Kindersley, 1993. ISBN 1-56458-314-7.
Carrots, marigolds, pumpkins, tigers, and goldfish are a few things that come in orange.

My Little Red Book. New York: Dorling Kindersley, 1993. ISBN 1-56458-313-9.
Color photographs of such familiar red things as strawberries, ladybugs, tomatoes, and fire trucks fill the pages.

My Little Yellow Book. New York: Dorling Kindersley, 1993. ISBN 1-56458-315-5.
This photographic book features the color yellow in daffodils, corn, lemons, cheese, pasta, and more.

Orange. Washington, D.C.: National Geographic Society, 1990.
An orange pumpkin starts the parade of orange things in this board book.

Pienkowski, Jan. *Colors*. New York: Little Simon, 1973, 1987. ISBN 0-671-68134-6.
This tiny board book includes a very simple introduction to colors.

Potter, Beatrix. *Benjamin Bunny's Colors*. Middlesex, England: Frederick Warne & Co., 1994. ISBN 0-7232-4118-X.
Benjamin Bunny and other Beatrix Potter characters tell all about colors.

Price, Sarah. *The Poky Little Puppy's Book of Colors*. Illustrated by Sarah Chandler. Racine, Wisconsin: Western Publishing Co., Inc., 1995. ISBN 0-307-12725-7.
As he plays, the Poky Little Puppy discovers colors all around him.

Puppy's Colors. Photographed by George Siede and Donna Preis. Lincolnwood, Illinois: Publications International, Ltd., 1994. ISBN 0-7853-0670-6.
As Puppy explores his world, he discovers all kinds of wonderful colorful things.

Purple. Washington, D.C.: National Geographic Society, 1990.
A butterfly, a snail, and a snake introduce the color purple.

Reasoner, Charles. *Color Crunch!* Los Angeles, California: Price, Stern, Sloan, 1996. ISBN 0-8431-3936-6.
A fabulous feast, including lavender jelly beans, yellow bananas, and pink bubble gum, fills the pages with a plethora of colors.

Red. Washington, D.C.: National Geographic Society, 1990.
A little red bird feeds its baby in this simple tale.

Ricklen, Neil. *Baby's Colors*. New York: Little Simon, 1990. ISBN 0-671-69539-8.
Babies and toddlers are dressed in colors in this sturdy board book.

Rizzo, Fran. *Colors*. New York: Modern Publishing. 1982, 1993. ISBN 0-87449-174-6. A small lion explores the world of colors in this simple board book.

St. Pierre, Stephanie. *Bunny's Easter Basket*. New York: Grosset & Dunlap, 1994. ISBN 0-448-40461-3.
Bunny looks for places to hide his colorful eggs in this small pop-up book.

Scarry, Richard. *Richard Scarry's Color Book*. New York: Random House, 1976. ISBN 0-394-83237-X.
Mr. Paint Pig travels all over town painting things for the townspeople.

Schulz, Charles M. *Snoopy's Crayons*. Columbus, Ohio: American Education Publishing, 1994. ISBN 1-56189-259-9.
As Snoopy plays with his crayons, he introduces colors and familiar objects.

Shapiro, Arnold. *Squiggly Wiggly's Surprise: A Finger Puppet Learns about Colors*. Los Angeles, California: Price, Stern, Sloan, 1975. ISBN 0-8431-0632-8.
Squiggly travels across the pages and encounters a colorful array of things.

Simeon, S. *Pink Drink: A Pop-Up Book of Color Rhymes*. Illustrated by Chris Reed. New York: Little Simon, 1995. ISBN 0-671-89833-7.
This bright and bouncy pop-up book includes a green bean, red bed, and blue shoe in its list of colorful rhymes.

Smith, Mavis. *Colors*. New York: Artists & Writers Guild Books, 1994. ISBN 0-307-17375-5.
Turn the wheel on each page to find the right color.

Szekeres, Cyndy. *Cyndy Szekeres' Colors*. Racine, Wisconsin: Western Publishing Co., Inc., 1992. ISBN 0-307-12167-4.
Baby animals in colorful attire dot the pages of this sturdy board book.

Tafuri, Nancy. *In a Red House*. New York. Greenwillow, 1987. ISBN 0-688-07185-6.
A young child tells all about the colorful things found in his blue room in his red house.

Tallarico, Tony. *Colors*. New York: Tuffy Books, 1982. ISBN 0-89828-304-3.
All the colors in an artist's palette are featured in a Tuffy tote board book.

Thomas the Tank Engine Colors. Illustrated by Pam Posey. New York: Random House, 1991. ISBN 0-679-81646-1.
Thomas and his friends show off their colors in this sturdy board book.

Tildes, Phyllis Limbacher. *Baby Animals Black and White*. Watertown, Massachusetts: Charlesbridge Publishing, 1998. ISBN 0-88106-3134.
Striking black and white images are used to show baby animals' faces in this wordless board book.

Tiny Toons Adventures First Book of Colors. New York: Heinemann, 1992. ISBN 0-434-96043-8.
As the Tiny Toons characters work and play, they display a variety of colors.

Tucker, Sian. *Colors*. New York: Little Simon, 1992. ISBN 0-671-76907-3.
A simple repetitive pattern and brightly colored pictures introduce colors.

Van der Meer, Ron, and Atie Van der Meer. *Funny Shoes: A Lift-the-Flap Color Book with a Surprise Gift*. New York: Aladdin Books, 1994. ISBN 0-689-71823-3.
Zany colorful shoes are on the feet of some very strange creatures in this unusual book.

Voss, Gisela. *Museum Colors*. Boston, Massachusetts: Museum of Fine Arts, 1993. ISBN 0-87846-369-0.
Works of art introduce colors and art to the young reader.

Vulliamy, Clara. *Blue Hat Red Coat*. Cambridge, Massachusetts: Candlewick Press, 1994. ISBN 1-56402-361-3.
One by one, a baby removes his colorful clothes.

Weiss, Ellen. *Baby Kermit's Color Book*. Illustrated by Lauren Attinello. Racine, Wisconsin: Western Publishing Co., 1993. ISBN 0-307-12539-4.
Baby Kermit and his friends introduce thirteen familiar colors.

Whalin, Gaylyn Williams. *God Made Colors*. Illustrated by Don Page. Wilton, Connecticut: Nelson, 1994. ISBN 0-7852-7817-6.
This small board book introduces colors along with some Bible friends, including Moses and his red flames and Jonah and the blue whale.

What Color Is It? Illustrated by Pamela Cote. Boston: Houghton Mifflin Co., 1997. ISBN 0-395-85909-3.
A parade of piglets prance across the pages, introducing colors.

Yellow. Washington, D.C.: National Geographic Society, 1990.
As the sun rises, all kinds of yellow things come alive in the pages of this board book.

Ziefert, Harriet. *Bear's Colors*. Illustrated by Susan Baum. New York: HarperCollins, 1993. ISBN 0-694-00454-5.
Bear introduces the familiar colors of ordinary objects.

Ziefert, Harriet. *Play Colors*. New York: DK Publishing, 1996. ISBN 0-7894-0711-6.
From a purple fish to a green turtle, children can match the Velcro-backed play pieces to the shape on the page.

Zoo Colors. New York: Little Simon, 1994. ISBN 0-671-86600-1.
Colorful animals in the zoo introduce colors in this board book.

Shapes

Albee, Sarah. *Allegra's Shapes*. Illustrated by Peter Panas. New York: Little Simon, 1996. ISBN 0-689-80843-7.
Allegra and her friends present a variety of colorful shapes, including rectangles and diamonds.

Baby Mickey's Book of Shapes. Racine, Wisconsin: Western Publishing Company, Inc., 1986. ISBN 0-307-10165-7.
While looking everywhere for his favorite toy, Baby Mickey encounters all sorts of shapes.

Barnes-Murphy, Rowan. *Shapes*. Nashville, Tennessee: Ideals Publishing Corporation, 1993. ISBN 0-8249-8606-7.
A mouse tries to find a shape to fit his mouse hole.

Bencraft, Gina. *Holiday Shapes*. Illustrated by Ray Mutimer. London: Michael O'Mara Books, Limited, 1995. ISBN 1-85479-791-3.
Bear Teacher has the class draw a picture using nine basic shapes.

Christmas Shapes. New York: Covent Garden Books, 1994. ISBN 1-56458-822-X.
From twinkling stars to rings of holly, the shapes of Christmas come alive in this tiny board book.

Clementson, John. *Spots on My Shoes*. New York: Studio Editions Limited, 1995. ISBN 0-15-200313-4.
Shapes and designs on familiar clothes are the basis of this simple board book.

Daniel, Frank. *Chanukah*. New York: Macmillan Publishing Co., 1993. ISBN 0-689-71733.
Squares and Chanukah are the subjects of this Jewish holiday board book.

Daniel, Frank. *Christmas*. New York: Macmillan Publishing Co., 1993. ISBN 0-689-71734-2.
Christmas introduces circles in this board book.

Daniel, Frank. *Halloween*. New York: Macmillan Publishing Co., 1993. ISBN 0-689-71736-9.
Pumpkins, skeletons, and witches shape up with triangles in a special holiday book.

Daniel, Frank. *Thanksgiving*. New York: Macmillan Publishing Co., 1993. ISBN 0-689-71735-0.
Semicircles and Thanksgiving have much in common in this American holiday board book.

Disney's Pop-Up Book of Shapes. Los Angeles, California: Disney Press, 1991. ISBN 1-56282-019-2.
Mickey and the gang discover the magic and fun of shapes.

Elliot, Rachel. *Goria's Book of Shapes*. Illustrated by Richard Walz. New York: McClanahan Book Company, Inc., 1995. ISBN 1-56293-533-X.
Goria takes a walk in the park and sees many different monster shapes.

Faulkner, Keith. *Tom's School Day: A Tiny Tom Book of Shapes*. Illustrated by Jonathan Lambert. New York: Cartwheel Books, 1993. ISBN 0-590-46948-7.
Tom the cat discovers all kinds of shapes at school in this lift-the-flap book.

Fosberg, John. *Cookie Shapes*. New York: Little Simon, 1997. ISBN 0-689-81288-4.
Shapes of all sorts are revealed in cookies in this delectable book for preschoolers.

Gave, Marc. *Walt Disney's Pinocchio Fun with Shapes and Sizes*. Illustrated by John Kurz. New York: Golden Press, 1992. ISBN 0-307-12332-4.
Pinocchio and his friends introduce shapes and sizes.

Henley, Claire. *Playshapes*. New York: Grosset & Dunlap, 1997. ISBN 0-448-41628-X.
This interactive board book includes four colorful plastic blocks to help preschoolers learn about shapes.

Hill, Eric. *Spot Looks at Shapes*. New York: G. P. Putnam's Sons, 1986. ISBN 0-399-21350-3.
Popular pooch Spot shows off some of his things, which come in a variety of shapes.

Lamut, Sonja. *Shapes*. New York: Grosset & Dunlap, 1997. ISBN 0-448-41632-8.
Children can spin the wheel and explore different shapes.

Learn-a-Round Shapes. Illustrated by Sue Cony. New York: McClanahan Book Company, Inc., 1991. ISBN 1-56293-149-0.
Shapes of all kinds are featured on these colorful pages.

Mayer, Mercer. *Little Critter Shapes*. New York: Random House, 1992. ISBN 0-679-87357-0.
Little Critter and his friends introduce different shapes as they play.

Murphy, Chuck. *My First Book of Shapes*. New York: Scholastic, 1992. ISBN 0-590-46303-9.
Tiny mice introduce shapes and encourage the reader to lift-the-flap to discover what appears in each shape.

P.B. Bear's Shapes. New York: DK Publishing, 1996. ISBN 0-7894-1422-8.
A small teddy bear shares a variety of shapes.

Pienkowski, Jan. *Shapes*. New York: Little Simon, 1989. ISBN 0-671-68135-4.
Familiar shapes are introduced as solitary units and as a part of familiar scenes in this board book.

Potter, Beatrix. *Learn with Jemima Puddle-Duck: A Book of Shapes*. Avenel, New Jersey: Derrydale Books, 1993. ISBN 0-517-07699-3.
Jemima Puddle-Duck searches for a new house with just the right shapes.

Puppy Round and Square. Illustrated by Norman Gorbaty. New York: Little Simon, 1991. ISBN 0-671-74436-4.
As puppies frolic and play, they find shapes all around them.

Rizzo, Fran. *Shapes*. New York: Modern Publishing, 1982, 1993. ISBN 087449-179-7.
A puppy leads the reader to all kinds of shapes and a surprise birthday party.

Rodman, Edmon J. *Snack Pack Books*. Illustrated by Ted and Linda Bick. Boston, Massachusetts: Little, Brown & Co., 1995. ISBN 0-316-15241-2.
Three small cereal boxes with pop-up books inside them show off shapes.

Ross, Tony. *Shapes*. San Diego, California: Red Wagon Books/Harcourt Brace & Co., 1994. ISBN 0-15-200319-3.
A little princess discovers the world is made up of shapes.

Santomero, Angela C. *The Shape Detectives*. Illustrated by Karen Craig. New York: Simon and Schuster, 1998. ISBN 0-689-81747-9.
Readers must search for shapes all around Blue's house in this lift-the-flap board book.

Secret Shapes: A Changing Picture Book. New York: Dorling Kindersley, 1995. ISBN 1-56458-962-5.
Pull the tab, and discover the secret behind the triangle, the cone, and other shapes.

Seeing Shapes. Designed by Barbara Sullivan; photography by Geoff Dann and Mort Engel. New York: Dutton, 1994. ISBN 0-525-45476-4.
This toddler board book shows what shapes are all around us.

Shapes. New York: Snapshot, 1994. ISBN 1-56458-536-0.
Photographs of real objects are used to show off shapes of all sorts.

Shapes. Philadelphia: Running Press, 1996. ISBN 1-56138-709-6.
The child matches the shape to the picture on each page.

Shapes Galore. New York: Snapshot, 1995. ISBN 0-7894-0231-9.
Objects from triangular napkins to squares of fabrics introduce shapes.

Shapiro, Arnold. *Circles*. Pictures by Bari Weissman. New York: Dial Press, 1992. ISBN 0-8037-1144-1.
This circular board book features things that are round.

Shapiro, Arnold. *Squares*. Pictures by Bari Weissman. New York: Dial Press, 1992. ISBN 0-8037-1146-8.
Simple text introduces things with four equal sides.

Shapiro, Arnold. *Triangles*. Pictures by Bari Weissman. New York: Dial Press, 1992. ISBN 0-8037-1147-6.
Turn the pages and discover all kinds of triangular-shaped objects.

Silverman, Maida. *Baby's Book of Shapes*. Illustrated by Kate Gleeson. Racine, Wisconsin: Western Publishing Company, Inc., 1992. ISBN 0-307-06063-2.
Bears, bunnies, and kittens are a few of the colorful animals who introduce shapes.

Smith, Mavis. *Circles*. New York: Warner, 1991. ISBN 1-55782-366-9.
Watch the sun change to egg yolks then to ornaments as children learn how circular objects are all around us.

Smith, Mavis. *Crescents*. New York: Warner, 1991. ISBN 1-55782-567-7.
The reader finds crescents in all sorts of familiar objects, including a feather, a crab's claw, and even a puppy's tail.

Smith, Mavis. *Shapes*. New York: Artists & Writers Guild Book, 1994. ISBN 0-307-17377-1.
Turn the wheel and find the correct shape.

Smith, Mavis. *Squares*. New York: Warner, 1991. ISBN 1-5782-364-2.
This simple board book introduces the concept of squares in the world around us.

Stortz, Diane. *My First Book of Shapes*. Illustrated by Jan Rice. Ashland, Ohio: Landoll, Inc., 1993. ISBN 1-56987-028-4.
A clever clown and his small friends introduce shapes.

Szekeres, Cyndy. *Cyndy Szekeres' Teeny Mouse Plays with Shapes*. Racine, Wisconsin: Western Publishing Co., Inc., 1994. ISBN 0-307-06088-8.
Teeny Mouse shows some of her toys and their different shapes.

Thomas the Tank Engine Shapes and Sizes. Illustrated by Deborah Colvin Borgo. New York: Random House, 1991. ISBN 0-679-81643-7.
Thomas introduces basic sizes and shapes in this small board book.

Tiny Toons Adventures First Book of Shapes. New York: Heinemann, 1992. ISBN 0-434-96044-6.
The Tiny Toons characters introduce a variety of shapes as they play.

Voss, Gisela. *Museum Shapes*. Boston, Massachusetts: Museum of Fine Arts, 1993. ISBN 0-87846-368-2.
This memorable board book focuses on shapes in works of art.

Wegman, William. *Triangle, Square, Circle*. New York: Hyperion Books, 1995. ISBN 0-7868-0104-2.
The famous Wegman dogs (Fay and family) show off basic shapes.

Whalin, Gaylyn Williams. *God Made Shapes*. Illustrated by Don Page. Wilton, Connecticut: Nelson, 1994. ISBN 0-7852-7818-4.
Arks, jewels, and bread are among the objects that introduce shapes and Bible friends.

White, Stephen. *Baby Bop Discovers Shapes*. Illustrated by Larry Daste. Allen, Texas: Barner Publishing, 1993. ISBN 1-57064-010-6.
Baby Bop invites the reader to help her find shapes.

Ziefert, Harriet. *Bear's Shapes*. Illustrated by Susan Baum. New York: HarperCollins, 1993. 0-694-00456-1.
Pizza, cheese, flags, and kites are only a few of the shapes Bear discovers.

Ziefert, Harriet. *Play Shapes*. New York: DK Publishing, 1996. ISBN 0-7894-0584-9.
A circle turns into a ladybug's spot, a diamond becomes a clown's eye—anything is possible with shapes in this intriguing board book.

Colors and Shapes

Colors and Shapes. Illustrated by Philip Hawksley. New York: McClanahan Book Company, Inc., 1994. ISBN 1-56293-429-5.
Match the picture on the wheel to those on the pages and learn about colors and shapes.

Henley, Claire. *Colors and Shapes: A First Lift-the-Flap Book*. New York: Silver Dolphin, 1996. ISBN 1-57145-055-6.
Hidden pictures and flaps help the reader discover shapes and colors.

Lacome, Julie. *Funny Business*. New York: Tambourine Books, 1991. ISBN 0-688-10159-3.
The canine clowns perform an array of merry tricks in this pop-up book.

Mayer, Mercer. *Old Howl Hall: Big Lift-and-Look Book*. New York: Random House, 1996. ISBN 0-679-88019-4.
Moose Mummy has a barrel of fun inside Old Howl Hill.

My First Book of Shapes and Colors. Illustrated by Ian Winton. New York: Little Simon, 1995. ISBN 0-671-51119-X.
Basic shapes and colors can be identified in a variety of objects.

Snow, Alan. *What Color Is It? What Shape Is It?* Wilton, Connecticut: Wishing Well Books, 1988. ISBN 0-88705-583-4.
By pushing and pulling handles on the pages, the reader easily identifies the different shapes and colors.

Taylor, Kate. *Colors, Shapes & Numbers*. New York: Bedrick/Blackie, 1992. ISBN 0-87226-505-6.
Kittens cavort across the pages and introduce all sorts of beginning concepts to the very young.

Van Fleet, Matthew. *Fuzzy Yellow Ducklings*. New York: Dial Books, 1995. ISBN 0-8037-1759-8.
Every page is a surprise when textured shapes turn into colorful creatures.

Van Fleet, Matthew. *Spotted Yellow Frogs*. New York: Dial Books, 1998. ISBN 0-8037-23504.
Shapes, patterns, and colors are the topic of this boldly illustrated concept book.

BOARD BOOK ACTIVITIES

Share *Red Strawberry* by John Clementson with older children. Select five foods and create a board book using the same cut paper collage and simple text found in the book.

After sharing *Color Crunch!* and other colorful food books, discuss the delicious foods mentioned in the books. Make a list of even more colorful treats.

Use *Color Crunch!* with older students (primary/elementary age). Make a chart showing all the foods found in the book. Take a poll of which food is the favorite of students in the class and record the data on the chart. Compare boys' and girls' favorite choices. Give students a copy of the foods in the chart, so they may ask their parents or other adults about their favorite foods. Use the data collected to make graphs and charts that compare and contrast foods. Discuss how colors may or may not play a role in favorite foods. Include a discussion about various methods of data collection and recording. Another way to approach the charts is to divide the class into groups, with each group assigned a specific color. The groups survey classmates, other students, and adults about their favorite foods in a particular color. Chart the results and discuss the role of color in food selection.

After sharing *Ice Cream Colors* with the children, create your own ice cream treats using different flavors and colors. Let the children make ice cream cones using two different colored flavors. If using real ice cream is not possible, then give the activity sheet, "Colorful Cones," so that each child can color a cone.

Divide the group into pairs for this activity. Give each child a piece of sidewalk chalk and a large piece of paper. Each child must trace the shape of his or her partner on the paper and then add details to complete the life-size drawing. Or do the shape tracings on the sidewalk.

Play "I Spy." Tell the children that you are thinking of a color and then give them some clues. When someone guesses correctly, it becomes his or her turn.

After sharing Tana Hoban's *Black on White* and *White on Black*, brainstorm a list of white or black objects. On a chalkboard or large writing pad, form a column for each color.

Help Mr. Paint Pig paint the town by giving each child the activity sheet, "Painting the Town," which goes with *Richard Scarry's Color Book*.

Share *Funny Shoes* with the children. Afterward, have them each make a set of paper shoes like those included with the book. Everyone takes home their own pair of "funny shoes."

Distribute the activity sheet, "Feel the Animals," to students, so they may create their own tactile color or shape pictures like those in *Fuzzy Yellow Ducklings*.

Make your own colorful ice cream cones. Color the ice cream scoops different colors and then describe what flavors make an irresistible treat for you.

Help Mr. Paint Pig paint things in Busytown. What colors should he use today? Color the paint cans, write the name of the color on the can, and tell what kind of object Mr. Paint Pig might paint with each color.

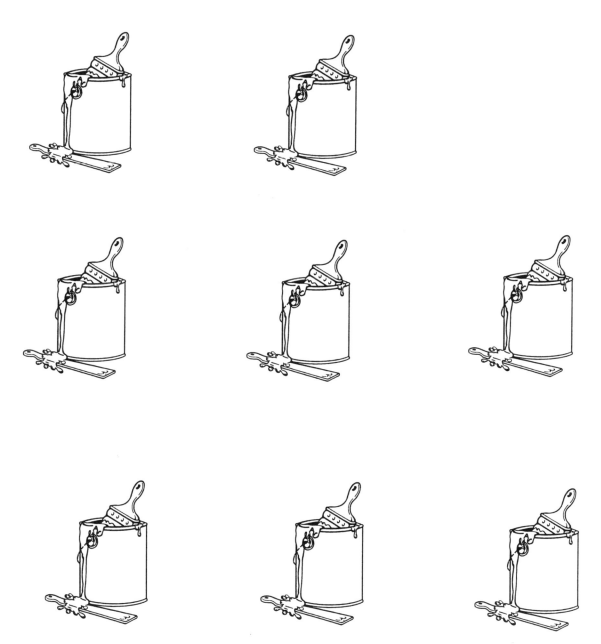

Feel the Animal

Use scraps of fabric, fur, suede, cotton, sandpaper, and other materials to make your picture of an animal that shows its coat. Combine a shape and color that together makes up a familiar animal. Write a three-word description of your animal.

3

ANIMALS IN COLOR AND SHAPE BOOKS

Of all the subjects used in books, animals are one of the most popular. Dogs, bears, cats, rabbits, and even bugs entertain the reader, provide information, and introduce such concepts as shapes and colors. The odd-shaped fish in Joanne and David Wylie's *A Fishy Shape Story* help familiarize children with shapes, whereas the assorted animals in *Brown Bear, Brown Bear, What Do You See?* by Bill Martin offer a look at colors. Animals are familiar, easily identified, and represent a sense of security and warmth. While animals are featured in many books discussed elsewhere, this chapter concentrates on animals as the central figures in a story as a means of identifying colors or shapes.

Perennial animal favorites such as dogs and cats are used frequently in color and shape books because they are children's common pets and represent security and comfort to children. Dogs are the central figures in two very good books on color, *What Color Is Caesar?* by Maxine Kumin and *Black Dog Red House* by Lizi Boyd. Caesar is a dalmatian who can't make up his mind about his colors. Should he be white with black spots or black with white spots? Caesar enlists the aid of his friends to help with the dilemma, but they only add to the confusion by introducing even more colors. Finally, with a little help from a magical friend, Caesar decides he likes all the colors of the rainbow and can be any color that he likes. While this story is a bit longer and geared toward upper elementary level, it is an excellent tale about making decisions and how colors are important in our lives.

Lizi Boyd offers a useful introduction to the idea of colors in *Black Dog Red House*. Black Dog and his friend explore the world of color inside and outside the red house. The black and white drawings have many angles and sharp edges to give the illustrations a stylish look. Only

the featured color is used as an accent to the black and white. On the edge of each double-page spread is a triangle that shows a rainbow of the colors used thus far in the text. Boyd uses both familiar colors, such as red and blue, as well as less familiar colors, such as magenta and turquoise. This book has a comforting ending that ties together all the colors when the dog and the boy take a nap under a multicolored quilt.

Rowan Barnes-Murphy offers cats, cats, and more cats in *Colors*. The zany cats get together to discuss what color to paint a mouse. The cats know all about the primary colors of red, blue, and yellow, and they show the reader how mixing one color with another will result in a third color. The text is very simple in this toddler-sized board book, and it easily explains the difficult concept of primary and secondary colors in only a few words. Bright cheerful illustrations of these comic cats make this a title for all ages. Only two kittens are mixing colors in the ageless story, *The Color Kittens* by Margaret Wise Brown. They try to make the color green, but instead, they manage to create a rainbow of colors and plenty of fun in the process. The illustrations offer a soft whimsical look at colors, but at the same time the objects in the featured colors are presented very realistically. First published in 1949, this story is still a delightful way to introduce colors, mixing colors, and familiar things in each color. In addition to the large Golden Book edition, this title is also a board book and a sound book.

When the cat's away, the mice come out to play, and mice are the focus of the next series of books. In *Shapes* by Rowan Barnes-Murphy, a tiny mouse tries to find a shape that will fit his mouse hole. Unbeknownst to the small mouse, a cat is nearby licking his lips in anticipation of a tasty meal. One by one, the mouse tries a variety of shapes only to discover that they do not fit. As the mouse tosses the shape aside, it hits the cat and stops him from pouncing. Finally, a semicircle fits the hole just in time to thwart the cat's attempt to catch some lunch. The simple repetitive text and humorous illustrations make *Shapes* a board book for all ages.

Cat-and-mouse games are also found in *Mouse Paint* by Ellen Stoll Walsh. When three white mice discover jars of red, blue, and yellow paint, they experiment. As they frolic in the color jars, a hungry cat lurks in the background. First, they fall into the jars one by one, but somehow, along the way, as they jump, dance, and play in the paint puddles, they discover amazing things happen when colors are mixed. Finally, they wash off the sticky paint and return to their original white color just in time to fool the waiting cat. The cut-paper collage illustrations in this wonderful cat-and-mouse story are simple, brilliant designs, which are very effective in introducing colors.

The Colors by Monique Felix features only one tiny mouse who finds some tubes of paint, an artist palette, and some brush. His curiosity overcomes him, and he sets out to create a masterpiece. At first, he is careful, only opening one tube at a time and experimenting with the primary colors. But that soon changes as he begins to mix colors to make more colors and succeeds in creating a terrible mess. The wordless story ends with the mouse and his mess, but the discussion can continue with ideas on what happens next, how the colors combine in new and unusual ways, and even how to clean up a paint mess. *The Colors* is from a series of "Mouse Books" designed to spark imagination, create interest, and foster verbal skills. This particular title fulfills the goals of the series as it introduces color concepts to readers.

Although introducing color concepts was not the original purpose of *Seven Blind Mice,* Ed Young integrates colors well into his adaptation of the Indian fable, "The Blind Men and the Elephant." When a strange Something appears at the pond, the seven blind mice speculate on what it could be. On each day of the week, the blind mice go out one by one to investigate the mysterious creature. Each colorful mouse describes what he found, but only from the part of the strange Something that he touched. Finally the seventh mouse, the white one, decides to settle the identity question once and for all. She runs across the "thing" in all directions and discovers why all the

mice had different descriptions. In the end the mice learn that it is important to look at things as a whole instead of just parts. The descriptions from each mouse evoke some unusual mental images. Young uses a black background with white borders on the pages with simple cut-paper collage designs on top of the black. While this Caldecott Honor Book is not a how-to book on colors, it certainly offers a story where colors are an integral part of the plot.

Jonathan Mouse by Ingrid Ostheeren is another story where color is simply a part of the story and not the focus of the book. A fairy casts a spell on Jonathan, which dooms him to turn the same color as the food that he eats. He turns red when he eats tomatoes, bright orange from carrots, and green from lettuce; but the worst is when he turns blue from the forget-me-nots that he eats. It is only with the help of his clever friends that Jonathan is able to finally break the spell. Rich, vivid colors fill the pages of this amusing tale of friendship designed for readers of all ages.

Turning colors also is the theme used in *Picasso the Green Tree Frog* by Amanda Graham. This simple story uses colors as a backdrop for the tale and not as a means of introducing and identifying a concept. When Picasso falls into a jar of jelly beans, he turns from his familiar green skin into a rainbow of colors. No matter what he does, the bright jelly bean colors just won't go away. It is only by accident that Picasso discovers that by eating the jelly beans color by color that he will finally return to normal (or so he thinks). The surprise ending and the simple story line makes *Picasso the Green Tree Frog* a good read-aloud book to share with listeners of any age.

From black and white to red and brown, bears can be found in both color and shape books. In *Red Bear* and *Red Bear's Fun with Shapes,* Bodel Rikys shows how much fun Red Bear has discovering colors and shapes all around him. Both books have very simple text, usually only the identification of the color or shape. The color or shape is shown as it naturally appears in Red Bear's everyday world, such as a triangle sandwich, an oval egg, or the crescent moon. Harriet Ziefert has a similar pair of bear books on colors and shapes that includes simple illustrations, little text, and familiar objects. In the board books, *Bear's Shapes* and *Bear's Colors,* a brown bear introduces ordinary objects to beginning readers. In still another set of board books (*A Week of*

Colours and *Holiday Shapes* by Gina Bencraft), a bear teacher and bear students learn all about colors and shapes in the world around them. In *A Week of Colours,* every day is a color day concluding with a big party on Sunday, when a rainbow appears over the school. The same bears and school are used in *Holiday Shapes,* but this time the Bear teacher has the class draw pictures of their holiday using any or all of nine basic shapes. One last bear book that is particularly appealing is *Mr. Panda's Painting* by Anne Rockwell. Mr. Panda is an artist who buys new tubes of paint for his next masterpiece. On the way home, he encounters all sorts of colorful things that match his paint tubes, such as yellow daffodils, green trees, and orange construction materials. He decides that his neighborhood is a colorful place to live, and he paints a picture of the very things that he saw on his way home. Rockwell's book offers an opportunity to learn more about artists and their tools (e.g., easels, brushes, and paints) as well as providing an entertaining story.

One of the most beloved children's books of all time, *Brown Bear, Brown Bear, What Do You See?* by Bill Martin, Jr., introduces all sorts of colorful animals, including a big brown bear. First published in 1967, the singsong text and Eric Carle's large, bold collage pictures have made this title a popular one with several generations of children. Martin uses a repetitive question-and-answer pattern in the text. The title question is put to the big brown bear who identifies a redbird looking at him. In turn, the question is directed to the redbird who sees a yellow duck, who sees a blue horse, and on and on and on. Children quickly pick up the pattern and chime in the answer by identifying the color and the animal that comes next. *Brown Bear, Brown Bear, What Do You See?* is filled with unforgettable images of some endearing creatures and text that reverberates in memory long after the pages are shut.

I Went Walking by Sue Williams uses a similar repetitive pattern to tell the story of a little boy on a walk. All kinds of colorful animals follow the boy until he makes his way home. Just like Martin's *Brown Bear, Brown Bear . . . ,* Williams uses a rhymthic pattern and cumulative folktale style to help children quickly grasp the plot and concentrate on the colors. One double-page spread uses the text "I went walking" on the left side followed by "What did you see?" on the right. Turn the page, and discover what colorful

animal that the boy sees looking at him. The pattern goes all through the book until the boy is followed by all the colorful animals he encounters including a black cat, red cow, and pink pig. These two books are wonderful companion volumes to use for talking about colors and rhyming patterns.

Jumping from bears to rabbits, Alan Baker offers an interesting look at colors and shapes from a rabbit's perspective in two books. In *White Rabbit's Color Book,* a soft, fluffy white rabbit finds three pots of paint (red, yellow, and blue) that look so inviting, he decides to jump in. As the bunny hops from paint pot to paint pot, he finds himself changing colors as the paint blends together. Finally he ends up a brown bunny, satisfied that he has tried to solve the mystery of which color is best. By using this book with Walsh's *Mouse Paint,* even young readers are able to get a sense of how primary colors combine to create more colors. A brown rabbit is the featured character in *Brown Rabbit's Shape Book.* When a package arrives for Brown Rabbit, his curiosity leads him to unwrap it immediately. The box is filled with balloons that the rabbit blows up into all sorts of shapes, such as oval, circle, and pear. Baker introduces shapes immediately with triangles on the wrapping paper, a square box, a card in the shape of a rectangle, and a boxful of balloons in all sorts of shapes. The illustrations in both books are in rich, vibrant colors with white, uncluttered backgrounds. Baker offers a three-dimensional look at curious rabbits exploring their worlds and the colors and shapes that fill it.

Chameleons, bees, and dragons are the subjects of other colors books. In *A Color of His Own* by Leo Lionni, a chameleon is tired of always changing colors and decides to go on a search for a color of his very own. Along the way he meets another chameleon and discovers that friendship and a sense of self-esteem is more important than a search for color. As always, Lionni manages to use beautiful collage illustrations and a simple story line to convey an important message. Colors are an accompaniment to the story, not the central focus. Chameleons are the focus of *A Million Chameleons* by James Young. Chameleons cavort across the pages and through numerous locations, changing colors and having fun wherever they go. They visit the zoo, climb trees, and even ride a carousel in their quest for fun. Bright, cheerful illustrations and rhyming text throughout the book inspire the reader to turn the pages to see what color the chameleons will choose next. Young combines color identification, a simple story, and a guessing rhyme game into a delightful story tale.

Colors, patterns, and changes are the focus of *Dragon Franz* by Elizabeth Shub. Franz is a very unhappy dragon with a big problem with colors. While the identification of various colors is not the intent of the author, colors are very much a part of the plot of this book. Poor Franz is the only dragon around who cannot spit fire, and no matter how hard he tries, fire never appears. Instead Franz has a special talent of his own. He can think about any color or design and his skin changes to the color or pattern that he is thinking about. Children are exposed to all sorts of vibrant colors and designs when Franz changes his skin, but perhaps the most important message of this book is about using the talents that you have been blessed with and believing in yourself.

Lisa Campbell Ernest describes the entire plot of her book in the title, *A Colorful Adventure of the Bee Who Left Home One Monday Morning and What He Found Along the Way*. This inquisitive bee takes wing from his hive to see what he can find. During his day of adventure, the bee finds green clover, purple flowers, blue sky, and other colorful wonders before returning to his yellow hive. The text is virtually wordless with only the color identified. The simple, bold, silkscreen images offer a clear, concise look at colors as seen in familiar things.

Bugs seem to go hand in hand with bees, and the master of the bug books, David Carter, has created a fascinating look at bugs, bugs, and more bugs in *Colors and Shapes*. Designed as an interactive learning tool for preschoolers, Carter uses easy-to-read text, lively illustrations, and fifty reusable vinyl bug stickers. The colorful bugs can be placed on pages and removed over and over again. The bugs come in all sorts of shapes and colors including heart bugs, purple grape bugs, triangle tree bugs, red tulip bugs, and even blue berry bugs. The sticker bug book even includes a place in the back to store the bugs.

Many other books about colors, shapes, and animals include more than one single species in them. The Little Giants First series by Alan Rogers includes four very easy-to-read titles for the beginner reader. Each of the four books focuses on one colorful animal and his quest. In *Red Rhino,* the rhino has trouble finding his red

balloon among all the red objects that he sees. In *Blue Tortoise,* once again the tortoise finds himself pitted against the Blue Rabbit in a race to the finish. All four in this series offer the reader adventuresome yet simple plots, brightly colored pictures, and cartoon-like images that concentrate on one single color.

Cartoon-like animals can be found in both the shape and color books by Marianna Mayer and Gerald McDermott. The Brambleberrys are a family of cute, lighthearted animals who introduce basic concepts in a fun and entertaining way. In *The Brambleberry's Animal Book of Color,* Panda shares all the colors of the rainbow as he and his friends set out to paint a picture. As they carry their supplies to the top of a hill, they encounter colorful things along the way, including a green pond, a sandy yellow beach, and a field of purple flowers. In *The Brambleberry's Animal Book of Big and Small Shapes,* Big Bear and Mouse introduce simple shapes in many sizes. Familiar objects, such as the sun, boxes, and eggs, reinforce the idea of shapes.

Brian Wildsmith concentrates on shapes in *Animal Shapes.* By using familiar animals, Wildsmith shows how they can be broken down into colorful shapes. The simple illustrations offer a dual look at familiar animals, such as a lion, elephant, goat, zebra, and anteater. On one side of the double-page spread is a colorful painting of an animal, while the facing page shows the same animal broken down in bold, colorful shapes. Wildsmith offers an interesting look at how shapes are put together to form a whole unit.

In *The Penguins Paint* by Valerie Tripp, the penguins decide that they are tired of their black-and-white lives. The text is simple, short rhyming sentences, with a soothing, satisfying ending. As the penguins try out colors one by one, the text describes what can be found in the color featured on each page. The Penguins paint their igloo different colors, but they cannot agree on a single color. Finally, the Penguins decide to paint a rainbow so that everyone is happy.

Two animal books center on folktales. *How the Birds Changed Their Feathers,* by Joanna Troughton, is a picture book based on a South American Indian tale. The folktale explains how birds came to have different colors. Patterned borders and rich, vibrant colors give the reader a sense of actually being in the jungle with the birds as they quarrel over the different colors. *How the Animals Got Their Colors,* by Michael

Rosen, is a collection of folktales about nature. One of the tales, an Ayoreo myth, is a creation myth about animals and colors. The Ayoreo Indians believe that heaven and earth were created by a sun god who changed humans into animals and then gave the animals their colors. The tale is illustrated with brilliant colors that accentuate how important colors are in our lives.

Because animals are so popular, they are very effective for teaching concepts like colors and shapes, for providing information, and for entertaining the reader. Oftentimes, an author can do all three of these tasks in the same story. From the simple, repetitive style of Bill Martin in *Brown Bear, Brown Bear, What Do You See?* to the misadventures of three mice in Ellen Stoll Walsh's *Mouse Paint,* an author provides a comforting tale with familiar, easily identified characters.

BIBLIOGRAPHY

Colors

Baker, Alan. *White Rabbit's Color Book*. New York: Kingfisher Books, 1994. ISBN 1-85697-953-9.
When rabbit finds three pots of paint, he tries to discover which color is the best.

Barnes-Murphy, Rowan. *Colors*. Nashville, Tennessee: Ideals Publishing Company, 1992. ISBN 0-8249-8530-3.
Zany cats discuss what color to paint a mouse.

Bencraft, Gina. *A Week of Colours*. Illustrated by Ray Mutimer. London: Michael O'Mara Books, Limited, 1995. ISBN 1-85479-771-9.
Every day is a special day for color at the bears' school.

Boyd, Lizi. *Black Dog Red House*. Boston, Massachusetts: Little, Brown and Company, 1993. ISBN 0-316-10443-4.
Black Dog and his boy friend explore colors inside and outside the red house.

Boynton, Sandra. *Blue Hat, Green Hat*. New York: Little Simon, 1984. ISBN 0-671-49320-5.
All the animals show off their clothes, but a small turkey can't get his on right.

Brown, Margaret Wise. *The Color Kittens*. Illustrated by Kathi Ember. Racine, Wisconsin: Western Publishing Co., Inc., 1949, 1994. ISBN 0-307-30217-2.
While trying to create green, two little kittens make a rainbow of colors.

Carle, Eric. *Hello Red Fox*. New York: Simon and Schuster, 1998. ISBN 0-689-81775-4.
Eric Carle uses clever eye tricks to introduce complementary colors in this story about the guests at Little Frog's birthday party.

Carroll, Kathleen Sullivan. *One Red Rooster*. Illustrated by Suzette Barbier. Boston, Massachusetts: Houghton Mifflin Company, 1992. ISBN 0-395-60195-9.
This counting tale introduces a host of noisy, colorful farm animals.

Charles, Donald. *Calico Cat Looks at Colors*. Chicago: Childrens Press, 1975. ISBN 0-516-03437-5. Formerly known as *Calico Cat's Rainbow*.
On one of his many adventures, Calico Cat demonstrates the colors of the rainbow.

Clifford, Eth. *Red Is Never a Mouse*. Illustrated by Bill Heckler. Indianapolis, Indiana: Bobbs-Merrill, Company, Inc., 1960.
Animals and their colors are the topic of this intriguing color book.

Cowley, Stewart. *Yellow Fish, Blue Fish*. Illustrated by Caroline Jayne Church. Wilton, Connecticut: Joshua Morris Books, 1994. ISBN 0-89577-597-2.
As a little girl watches through a tiny window, a parade of colorful fish swim by.

Ernst, Lisa Campbell. *A Colorful Adventure of the Bee Who Left Home One Monday and What He Found Along the Way*. Illustrated by Lee Ernst. New York: Lothrop, Lee and Shepard Books, 1986. ISBN 0-688-05563-X; 0-688-05564-8 (lib bdg).
A bee sets out on an adventure and passes by a variety of colors in nature before returning home.

Felix, Monique. *The Colors*. Columbus, Ohio: American Education Publishing, 1993. ISBN 1-56846-075-9.
When a tiny mouse discovers some tubes of paint, he sets out to create a masterpiece (or a mess?).

Gerstein, Mordecai. *Follow Me!* New York: William Morrow & Company, 1983. ISBN 0-688-01855-6; 0-688-01856-4 (lib bdg).
A flock of colorful ducks and geese get lost on their way home for dinner.

Godwin, Laura. *Little White Dog*. Illustrated by Dan Yaccarino. New York: Hyperion Books for Children, 1998. ISBN 0-7868-0297-9; 0-7868-2256-2 (lib bdg).
One by one the animals disappear and then reappear when the lights are turned on.

Graham, Amanda. *Picasso the Green Tree Frog*. Pictures by John Siow. Milwaukee, Wisconsin: Gareth Stevens Publishing, 1985. ISBN 1-55532-177-1; 1-55532-152-6.
When he falls into a jar of jelly beans, Picasso soon wishes his old green color would return.

Greenway, Shirley. *Color Me Bright*. Halesite, New York: Whispering Coyote Press, 1992. ISBN 1-879085-53-4.
Photographs of animals introduce colors.

Kumin, Maxine. *What Color Is Caesar?* Illustrated by Evaline Ness. New York: McGraw-Hill Book Company, 1978. ISBN 0-07-035638-6.
Caesar can't decide if he wants to be white with black spots or black with white spots.

Lionni, Leo. *A Color of His Own*. New York: Alfred A. Knopf, 1995. ISBN 0-679-84197-0; 0-679-94197-5 (lib bdg).
When a chameleon searches for a color of his own, he discovers happiness and a true friend.

Lopshire, Robert. *Put Me in the Zoo*. New York: Random House, 1960. ISBN 0-394-90017-0.
A large, yellow cat shows all the good things he can do, including changing the color of his spots.

McKissack, Patricia, and Frederick McKissack. *The Big Bug Book of Things to Do*. Illustrated by Bartholomew. St. Louis, Missouri: Milliken Publishing Company, 1987. ISBN 0-88335-766-6.

The big bugs have lots of fun things to do, but sometimes thinking about colors makes them feel special.

Martin, Bill, Jr. *Brown Bear, Brown Bear, What Do You See?* Pictures by Eric Carle. New York: Henry Holt and Company, 1967, 1983, 1996. ISBN 0-8050-0201-4; 0-8050-5019-1 (Board).
Repetitive text and bold, bright collage animals introduce colors.

Mayer, Marianna, and Gerald McDermott. *The Brambleberry's Animal Book of Color.* Honesdale, Pennsylvania: Bell Brooks, 1987. ISBN 1-878093-76-2.
Panda shares all the colors of the rainbow.

Ostheeren, Ingrid. *Jonathan Mouse.* Pictures by Agnes Mathieu. Translated by Rosemary Lanning. New York: North-South Books, 1985. ISBN 0-03-005848-1.
When a fairy casts a spell on Jonathan that turns him the color of whatever he eats, it takes some ingenuity to break the spell.

Packard, Mary. *My First Book of Colors.* Illustrated by Eleanor Wasmuth. New York: Checkerboard Press, 1987, 1992.
When Chameleon wants to play hide-and-seek, Frog and Toad aren't very happy about her ability to blend with the background.

Pinkwater, Daniel. *Bear's Picnic.* New York: E. P. Dutton, 1972, 1984. ISBN 0-525-44102-6.
When a bear paints a picture, two proper gentlemen question him about the things that he draws.

Poulet, Virginia. *Blue Bug's Book of Colors.* Illustrated by Peggy Perry Anderson. Chicago: Childrens Press, 1981. ISBN 0-516-03442-1.
Through trial and error, Blue Bug and his friend Nat discover how to mix colors to make more colors.

Pragoff, Fiona. *What Color?* New York: Bantam Doubleday Dell Pub., 1987. ISBN 0-385-24173-9.
Photographs of animals introduce colors.

Rikys, Bodel. *Red Bear.* New York: Dial Books, 1992. ISBN 0-8037-1048-8.
As Red Bear gets ready for the day, he discovers colors all around him.

Rockwell, Anne. *Mr. Panda's Painting.* New York: Macmillan Publishing Co., 1983. ISBN 0-02-777451-1.
When Mr. Panda buys new paint tubes, he decides to paint a picture of his neighborhood.

Rogers, Alan. *Blue Tortoise.* Milwaukee, Wisconsin: Gareth Stevens Publishing, 1990. ISBN 0-8368-0404-X.
Blue Tortoise and Blue Rabbit meet once again in a classic race.

Rogers, Alan. *Green Bear.* Milwaukee, Wisconsin: Gareth Stevens Publishing, 1990. ISBN 0-8368-0406-6.
Green Bear encounters many things in his favorite color.

Rogers, Alan. *Red Rhino.* Milwaukee, Wisconsin: Gareth Stevens Publishing, 1990. ISBN 0-8368-0406-6.
Red Rhino has trouble finding his red balloon among all the other red objects.

Rogers, Alan. *Yellow Hippo.* Milwaukee, Wisconsin: Gareth Stevens Publishing, 1990. ISBN 0-8368-0405-8.
Hippo takes a walk with a yellow wagon, placing all sorts of yellow objects in it.

Rogers, Margaret. *Green Is Beautiful.* Illustrated by Bernadette Watts. Windermere, Florida: Ray Rourke Publishing Co., Inc., 1982, 1977. ISBN 0-86592-128-8.
The jungle animals argue about which color is the most beautiful in the world.

Rosen, Michael. *How the Animals Got Their Colors.* Illustrated by John Clementson. San Diego, California: Harcourt Brace Jovanovich, 1992. ISBN 0-15-236783-7.
The Ayoreo Indian myth about animals and colors is among the folktales in this collection.

Saire, Diane. *Polka-Dot Puppy's Birthday: A Book about Colors.* Illustrated by Linda Hohag and Lori Jacobson. Chicago: Childrens Press, 1988. ISBN 0-516-05606-9; 0-516-45606-7 (pbk).
When Polka-Dot Puppy's friends give him a surprise birthday party, he matches each colorful present to one of his colorful friends.

Shub, Elizabeth. *Dragon Franz.* Pictures by Ursula Konopka. Adapted from the German. New York: Greenwillow Books, 1976. ISBN 0-688-80077-7.
Franz is unhappy about not being able to spit fire, but he finally discovers happiness with his real talent.

Szekeres, Cyndy. *Cyndy Szekeres' Colors.* Racine, Wisconsin: Western Publishing Company, 1992. ISBN 0-307-12167-4.
Baby animals in colorful attire dot the pages of this sturdy board book.

Tripp, Valerie. *The Penguins Paint.* Illustrated by Sandra Cox Kalthoff. Chicago: Childrens Press, 1987. ISBN 0-516-01567-2.
When the Penguins tire of their black-and-white land, they decide to add a little color.

Troughton, Joanna. *How the Birds Changed Their Feathers.* New York: Bedrick/Blackie, 1976. ISBN 0-216-90084-0.
A retelling of a South American Indian folktale about how birds came to be different colors.

Walsh, Ellen Stoll. *Mouse Paint.* San Diego, California: Harcourt, Brace & Co., 1989. ISBN 0-15-256025-4.
Three white mice experiment with jars of paint and discover some amazing things.

Williams, Sue. *I Went Walking.* Illustrated by Julie Vivas. San Diego, California: Gulliver Books/Harcourt Brace Jovanvich, 1989. ISBN 0-15-299471-8; 0-15-200771-7 (bd).

When a little boy takes a walk, he discovers animals in all kinds of colors.

Winograd, Deborah. *My Color Is Panda*. New York: Green Tiger Press, 1993. ISBN 0-671-79152-4.
A black-and-white panda tries to imagine what it would be like to be another color.

Wood, Jakki. *Moo, Moo, Brown Cow*. Illustrated by Rog Bonner. San Diego, California: Harcourt Brace Jovanovich, 1992. ISBN 0-15-200533-1.
A lively kitten visits the barnyard to ask all the mother animals about their babies.

Young, Ed. *Seven Blind Mice*. New York: Philomel Books, 1992. ISBN 0-399-22261-8.
Seven colorful blind mice set out to investigate a mysterious something by the pond.

Young, James. *A Million Chameleons*. Boston: Little, Brown & Co., 1990. ISBN 0-316-97129-4.

A million careful chameleons have a wonderful fun-filled day, changing colors everywhere they go.

Ziefert, Harriet. *Bear's Colors*. Illustrated by Susan Baum. New York: HarperCollins, 1993. ISBN 0-694-00454-5.
Bear introduces the familiar color of ordinary objects.

Zolotow, Charlotte. *Mr. Rabbit and the Lovely Present*. With color illustrations by Maurice Sendak. New York: Harper & Row Publishers, 1962.
A little girl asks Mr. Rabbit to help her find a birthday present for her mother.

Zoo Colors. New York: Little Simon, 1994. ISBN 0-671-86600-1.
Colorful animals in the zoo introduce colors in this board book.

Shapes

Baker, Alan. *Brown Rabbit's Shape Book*. New York: Kingfisher Books, 1994. ISBN 1-85697-950-4.
Brown Rabbit receives a package filled with some amazing shapes.

Barnes-Murphy, Rowan. *Shapes*. Nashville, Tennessee: Ideals Publishing Company, 1993. ISBN 0-8249-8606-7.
A mouse tries to find a shape to fit his mouse hole.

Bencraft, Gina. *Holiday Shapes*. Illustrated by Ray Mutimer. London: Michael O'Mara Books, Limited, 1995. ISBN 1-85479-791-3.
Bear Teacher has the class draw a picture using nine basic shapes.

Charles, Donald. *Calico Cat Looks at Shapes*. Chicago: Childrens Press, 1975. ISBN 0-516-03436-7.
Calico Cat discovers shapes all around him.

Henkes, Kevin. *Circle Dogs*. Illustrated by Dan Yaccarino. New York: Greenwillow Books, 1997. ISBN 0-688-15446-8; 0-688-15447-6 (lib bdg).
The reader spends a day with the circle dogs, who live in a square house with a square yard, eat circle snacks, and dig circle holes.

Mayer, Marianna, and Gerald McDermott. *The Bram-*

berry's Animal Book of Big and Small Shapes. Honesdale, Pennsylvania: Bell Books, 1987. ISBN 1-878093-77-0.
Big Bear and Mouse teach simple shapes.

Moncure, Jane Belk. *Ape Finds Shapes: A Book about Shapes*. Illustrated by Joy Friedman. Elgin, Illinois: The Child's World, 1988. ISBN 0-89565-917-0.
Tracy and her four ape friends look for shapes all around them.

Rikys, Bodel. *Red Bear's Fun with Shapes*. New York: Dial Books, 1993. ISBN 0-8037-1317-7.
Red Bear explores shapes both inside and outdoors.

Wildsmith, Brian. *Animal Shapes*. New York: Oxford University Press, 1980. ISBN 0-19-279733-6.
Familiar animals form colorful shapes.

Wylie, Joanne and David Wylie. *A Fishy Shape Story*. Chicago: Childrens Press, 1984.
This fishy story introduces a variety of shapes.

Ziefert, Harriet. *Bear's Shapes*. Illustrated by Susan Baum. New York: HarperCollins, 1993. ISBN 0-694-00456-1.
Pizza, cheese, flags, and kites are only a few of the shapes that Bear discovers.

Colors and Shapes

Carter, David A. *Colors and Shapes*. New York: Simon and Schuster, 1996. ISBN 0-689-81042-3.

Bugs, bugs, and more bugs show off their shapes and colors in this interactive sticker storybook.

Ask students to write another color adventure for the black dog and his small boy friend in *Black Dog Red House* by Lizi Boyd. What other things might they see in and around the red house? Have them write a story (individually or in small groups) by using another color for the house or another setting.

Using the activity sheet "What Color Should I Be?" have students help Caesar (*What Color Is Caesar?* by Maxine Kumin) decide what color he should be.

Mouse Paint by Ellen Stoll Walsh and *The Colors* by Monique Felix are two titles that complement one another. After sharing both stories with children, ask them to draw their own mouse and write about his color adventures.

For those with lots of courage, try feet painting like the mice in *Mouse Paint*. (DO THIS OUTSIDE.) Pour tempera paint into three large tubs. Each tub contains one of the primary colors (red, yellow, blue). Place white butcher paper nearby. Place a bare foot in one tub at a time, and then step on the paper making footprints. If you step one footprint on top of another, you can mix colors, just like the mice. Be sure to have lots of soapy water and towels ready for cleanup.

Divide the class into six groups, one for each of the colors used in *Mouse Paint* (Ellen Stoll Walsh). Have each group color square sheets of paper to hold up when their color is mentioned in the story.

To show the children how colors mix, combine a few drops of bleach and food coloring. Use an overhead projector to demonstrate color mixing to an entire class.

Use *The Colors* as a starting point to have students write about what happens to the mouse after he is all covered with paint. Imitate the style of Monique Felix by using only illustrations to tell the story.

I Went Walking by Sue Williams uses a repetitive pattern to tell a simple color story. Let students brainstorm a list of other actions that the little boy might have used. Use the activity sheet "I Went _____" to create your own predictable story about a walk.

After sharing *Picasso the Green Tree Frog* by Amanda Graham, have the entire group write another color adventure for Picasso. Let everyone munch on jelly beans as they think of things for Picasso. Be sure that each child contributes at least one sentence or idea toward the group story.

After reading *Brown Rabbit's Shape Book,* try making different shapes with balloons. Bring in a box of assorted balloons and let the children blow them up for different shapes. Compare the balloon shapes to familiar objects.

Hold your own "week of colors," just as the bears do in Gina Bencraft's book. Feature a color each day. Wear clothes in that color, share color foods, have color art, and so on.

Share the stories about chameleons (*A Million Chameleons* by James Young, *A Color of His Own* by Leo Lionni and *My First Book of Color* by Mary Packard). Discuss chameleons and their ability to camouflage themselves. Discuss how other animals such as the snow rabbit and walking stick use their colors to hide from enemies. Have the children research and report on other animals that use color as a disguise.

Pass out the activity sheet "Ever-Changing Chameleons" and ask students to color, draw, and write a brief rhyme about each one. Another activity is to sponge paint the chameleon and draw something that he is sitting on. Write a sentence explaining how the chameleon changed color to match the object he sat on. For example, a chameleon perched on an orange might turn orange.

After reading Lisa Campbell Ernst's tale of a colorful bee, write or tell another color adventure for the bee. Follow the pattern of Ernst's tale by only naming the color of the objects that the bee passes by. Older students might want to embellish their color adventures. Instead of using colors, have the bee go on a shape adventure and follow a similar story pattern of only naming the shape.

After sharing the Little Giants First series by Alan Rogers, ask students to write their own color stories about an animal and its adventure. They should choose a familiar animal and one color as the basis for the tale. Distribute the story starter sheet "Colorful Animals" as a guide.

Choose a familiar animal and, with students' help, break a picture of the animal into simple shapes, just as Brian Wildsmith does in his book, *Animal Shapes*. Have the class draw the animals following the pattern established by Wildsmith.

After sharing *A Fishy Shape Story* by Joanne and David Wylie, play a fishing game. Attach paper clips to a variety of shapes and place them in the center of a circle of children. Pass a pole with a magnet on the end around the circle and let each child fish for a shape. Assign each child a special shape to try to catch.

Have each child cut out a shape of some sort and use it to create a fish. Add tail, fins, and other details. Fill a wall with a school of fish.

After reading *Mr. Rabbit and the Lonely Present* by Charlotte Zolotow, have the class make a list of all the presents that Mr. Rabbit suggested. Discuss how the fruit basket was the perfect gift and all the colors that came in it. What other colorful fruits might have been added? Afterward, make a fruit salad to share with the children.

What Color Should I Be?

Help Caesar decide what color he should be by adding colors to his coat.

Instead of going on a walk, use another action verb to write a color story. Follow the repetitive pattern set up in the story, *I Went Walking,* by Sue Williams. Repeat the pattern as many times as you like. Illustrate your story when you are finished.

I WENT _____

(Action)

WHAT DID YOU SEE?

I SAW A _____

(Color)

_____ LOOKING AT ME.

(Object)

Color or paint the chameleon. Draw an object for the chameleon to sit on and write a brief rhyming sentence to describe how the chameleon changed.

Colorful Animals

Use the story starter as a framework for writing a simple animal story similar to the Little Giants First series by Alan Rogers. Choose a color and an animal to use in your story.

_____ _____ HAS A

          (Color)   (Animal)

_____ _____ TO PUT IN

          (Color)   (Object)

THE _____.

              (Name of object: wagon, car, etc.)

(What else did the animal find?)

4

RHYME AND RHYTHM THROUGH COLORS AND SHAPES

One of the most effective ways to teach any concept is using rhyme and music to catch students' attention. The simple beat of a song, the way that words flow quickly and easily, or the repetitive phrases in a poem make learning easier, faster, and fun. Even the smallest child will respond to the sound of music and rhythm, whether it be from a Mother Goose rhyme or a *Barney* song. From a very early age, children learn their alphabet and numbers from nursery rhymes and songs before moving on to a stage where they apply their knowledge of a concept to a real-life situation, such as reading or identifying colors and shapes. Whereas many stories use rhymes as a means of relating a tale, this chapter concentrates more on poetry and songs that emphasize the important role of colors and shapes in everyday life.

Perhaps the premier wizard of rhyming stories and nonsensical verse for children is Dr. Seuss. *Green Eggs and Ham* and *The Shape of Me and Other Stuff* might be considered simple nonsense stories rather than "concept" books; however, both titles are valuable for introducing the idea of colors and shapes with a quick bouncy rhyme. *Green Eggs and Ham* is a modern classic, and there are very few children who have not read this marvelous tale of Sam-I-Am, who tries to get his friend to sample a new taste treat. He offers all sorts of possible scenarios for trying the treat from "with a mouse" and "in a box" to "in the rain" and "on a boat." Finally, after numerous tries, his friend tries the green eggs and ham, and much to his amazement, he finds the unusual treat delicious. Seuss has created a wonderful tale to use in showing children that sometimes it is necessary to try new things to know if they are good. In *The Shape of Me and Other Stuff,* two children talk about all the different shapes that can be found around them. All sorts of shapes

found in balloons, bugs, spiderwebs, peanuts, and bees are discussed as the children look for shapes. The illustrations are silhouette drawings of shapes interspersed with white and colorful backgrounds and lettering. Both books are written in typical Seuss fashion, which pairs familiar objects and ideas with exagerrated rhymes and drawings.

Leonard Everett Fisher uses simple descriptive rhymes in his tale, *Boxes! Boxes!* The reader gets a glimpse into a child's room filled with boxes in all shapes and sizes. Boxes for pencils, candy, kites, and even jacks-in-the-box are explored in this unusual book about one specific shape. Bold, imaginative three-dimensional illustrations in rich vibrant colors decorate the pages. Fisher's concentration on boxes is a valuable title to use in discussing less familiar geometric shapes, such as cubes and cones.

Simple rhymes introduce colors in three beginner books. In *Colors,* a simple board book, Tedd Arnold uses familiar nursery rhymes that contain color words. The color word is highlighted in the rhyme as well as used for each page's background. Simple rhymes from some colorful animals are used in *Pink, Red, Blue, What Are You?* by Laura McGee Kvasnosky. As the comic animals strut across the pages, they use simple phrases to tell their colors. For example, the pigs say "We're pink. We stink." Other animals find appropriate rhymes for their colors. *Pink Drink: A Pop-Up Book of Color Rhymes* by S. Simeon uses a similar rhyming scheme. Each page uses the featured color as the background with word identification of the color. Open the flap on the page and up pops an object that rhymes with the color word. For the color green, up pops a big green bean stalk with Jack and the giant, while for white, a kite pops up off the page. This interesting pop-up book is useful for all ages as a color concept book and as a example of simple rhymes.

Several poets have used the idea of colors and the imagery associated with them as the basis for their work. In the classic title, *Hailstones and Halibut Bones,* Mary O'Neill wrote a series of lyrical poems celebrating colors. Each poem describes a color and some of the familiar things that are associated with the color. Color is best known by sight, but in these poems O'Neill fills the pages with rich language and vivid imagery that connects colors with the other senses so that a reader can almost taste, feel, hear, and smell a color. When O'Neill describes green, one can almost feel the coolness of a shady tree, smell the country breezes over green grass, and taste the sourness of olive green pickles. John Wallner's illustrations in the new edition of this classic work are filled with striking, colorful images that enhance the words that O'Neill makes come alive.

The renowned poet, Christina Rossetti, writes a vivid description of colors in her poem, *Colors.* The structure is very simple with only a questions posed, "What is _____?" Then she describes something in the color. While the poem can be found in many collections, the picture book rendition is more appropriate to use with children.

Arnold Adoff concentrates on only one color in *Greens.* Adoff uses twenty-six glorious poems to celebrate the color green and its role in a child's world. He covers green grass, dandelion greens, grasshoppers, garden hoses, leaves, and even Kermit the frog and the Loch Ness Monster. The watercolor illustrations and the happy verses celebrate the world of a child surrounded by "greens." *White Is the Moon* by Valerie Greeley offers short one-page poems that pair colors and animals in delicately illustrated nature scenes. Beginning with the white of the moon, each poem introduces a color and an animal, circling through the day and back to the moon at the end. A more detailed discussion of this book is included in the section on science.

Finally, there is *Out of the Blue: Poems about Colors* by Hiawyn Oram. Oram includes dozens of poems in his celebration of colors. Playful couplets, limericks, and longer verses explore the variety of shades that the English language gives to colors. Shades of the featured color are used as the background for the text and illustrations.

Oram's poetry covers a variety of topics that may describe a color, explain a color phrase or expression, or even tell a story. For the color red, he includes a poem called "Embarrassment," which captures the very essence of that particular feeling. He also uses a story poem, "Song of the Carnivore," to tell about a carnivore, who eats red meat. "White Elephants," "Yellow Soap," and "Green Cheese" are only a few of the topics in this fascinating collection of color poems.

Meredith Dunham concentrates on showing the words used to identify colors and shapes in different languages in her two books dealing with concepts. In *Colors: How Do You Say It?* each double page has a large square in the center of each page. On the left, each side of the square includes the pronunciation of the color and object in the four different languages. On the right, the square has a familiar object in the color along with the identification of the object in the four languages. In *Shapes: How Do You Say It?* Dunham uses the same layout, but shapes are used in the centers of the squares along with the pronunciation and identification in the four different languages.

In addition to poetry, color and shape rhymes are found in music and picture book renditions of songs. In *Mary Wore Her Red Dress and Henry Wore His Green Sneakers,* Merle Peek uses a old folk song that introduces colors. Katy Bear decides to have a birthday party and invite all of her animal friends. As each animal arrives, he or she is dressed in a different color and garment. Mary is in a red dress, Henry wears green sneakers, and Katy has a yellow sweater. The illustrations are filled with scenes of the birthday party, the games, and the birthday cake. The illustrations are very cleverly printed using only the colors that have been named thus far. As the song goes on, the pages become more and more colorful. Not only is this a wonderful way to introduce colors, but it is a delightful song and story.

Using poetry and songs to introduce colors and shapes is an effective way to reinforce concepts. The rhythm, repetitive language, and the vivid imagery can capture a child's imagination and turn learning into a delightful experience. From Dr. Seuss and his nonsense stories to the lyrical, colorful descriptions in *Hailstones and Hailbut Bones,* rhyme makes learning a pleasure.

BIBLIOGRAPHY

Colors

Adoff, Arnold. *Greens*. Illustrated by Betsy Lewin. New York: Lothrop, Lee and Shepard Books, 1988. ISBN 0-688-04276-7; 0-688-04277-5 (lib bdg).

Adoff celebrates the color green and its role in a child's world.

Arnold, Tedd. *Colors*. New York: Little Simon, 1985. ISBN 0-671-77825-0.

Arnold uses nursery rhymes that contain color words in this board book.

Carlstrom, Nancy White. *Hooray for Me Hooray for You Hooray for Blue: Jesse Bear's Colors*. Illustrations by Bruce Degen. New York: Little Simon, 1997. ISBN 0-689-802727-9.

In simple rhyming text, Carlstrom tells how Jesse Bear puts on a colorful play.

Dunham, Meredith. *Colors: How Do You Say It? English–French–Spanish–Italian*. New York: Lothrop, Lee and Shepard Books, 1987. ISBN 0-688-06948-7; 0-688-06949-5.

Colors are introduced using a variety of objects along with the appropriate descriptive words in four languages.

Greeley, Valerie. *White Is the Moon*. New York: Macmillan, 1991. ISBN 0-02-736915-3.

From night to day and back to night, these short poems introduce colors and animals.

Griffith, Neysa and Steve Durarte. Illustrated by Deborah Morse. New York: Enchante Pub.

The Magic of Blue. 1995. ISBN 1-56844-029-4.

The Magic of Green. 1995. ISBN 1-56844-028-6.

The Magic of Orange. 1995. ISBN 1-56844-026-X.

The Magic of Red. 1995. ISBN 1-56844-025-1

The Magic of Violet. 1994. ISBN 1-56844-031-6.

The Magic of Yellow. 1995. ISBN 1-56844-027-8.

Each title in this Magic of Color series concentrates on one color, using poetry and rhymes to tell about familiar objects in each color.

Herbst, Judith. *Festival of Colors*. Illustrated by Fabienne Boisnard. New York: Barron's Educational Series, Inc., 1991, 1995. ISBN 0-8120-6473-9.

Charming verses connect colors with familiar objects.

Kvasnosky, Laura McGee. *Pink, Red, Blue, What Are You?* New York: Dutton, ISBN 0-525-45233-8.

A parade of colorful animals strut across the pages of this simple rhyming book.

Lundell, Margaretta, retold by. *The Land of Colors*. Based on the Italian text by Tiziano Sclavi. Illustrated by Nadia Pazzaglia; graphics by Giorgio Vanetti. New York: Grosset and Dunlap, 1982. ISBN 0-448-21028-2.

Children can poke their fingers through the bright, round sun that shines on a red town, pink stage, yellow circus, and more.

O'Neill, Mary. *Hailstones and Halibut Bones*. Newly illustrated by John Waller. New York: Doubleday, 1961, 1989. ISBN 0-385-24484-3; 0-385-24485-1 (lib bdg); 0-385-41078-6.

Each poem in this classic collection describes a color and some of traits found in the color.

Oram, Hiawyn. *Out of the Blue: Poems about Color*. Illustrated by David McKee. New York: Hyperion Books for Children, 1993. ISBN 1-56282-470-8.

Elephants, soap, and cheese are only a few of the colorful topics found in this collection of verses.

Peek, Merle. *Mary Wore Her Red Dress and Henry Wore His Green Sneakers*. New York: Clarion Books/ Ticknor and Fields, 1985. ISBN 0-89919-324-2.

When Katy Bear has a birthday party, all of her friends wear a different color.

Ricklen, Neil. *My Colors—Mis Colores*. New York: Aladdin Books, 1994. ISBN 0-689-71772-5.

Colored photographs of children introduce colors in English and Spanish.

Rossetti, Christina. *Colors*. Pictures by Mary Teichman. New York: HarperCollins, 1992. ISBN 0-06-022626-9; 0-06-022650-1 (lib bdg).

Rossetti provides a simple introduction to colors in this picture book rendition of her classic poem.

Seuss, Dr. *Green Eggs and Ham*. New York: Random House, 1960. ISBN 0-394-80016-8; 0-394-90016-2 (lib bdg).

Sam-I-Am tries desperately to get his friend to try a special taste treat.

Simeon, S. *Pink Drink: A Pop-Up Book of Color Rhymes*. Illustrated by Chris Reed. New York: Little Simon, 1995. ISBN 0-671-89833-7.

This bright and bouncy pop-up book includes a green bean, red bed, and blue shoe in its list of colorful rhymes.

What Color? New York: Little Simon, 1992. ISBN 0-671-76930-8.

This simple board book introduces colors using both English and Spanish words.

Shapes

Dolplich, Rebecca. *What Is Round?* Photographs by Maria Ferrari. New York: Harper Festival, 1999. ISBN 0-694-01208-4.
A host of circular things are introduced in these easy-to-read poems.

Dunham, Meredith. *Shapes: How Do You Say It? English–French–Spanish–Italian*. New York: Lothrop, Lee and Shepard Books, 1987. ISBN 0-688-06952-5; 0-688-06953-3.
A variety of shapes are introduced, along with the same words translated in English, French, Spanish, and Italian.

Fisher, Leonard Everett. *Boxes! Boxes!* New York: Viking Press, 1984. ISBN 0-670-18334-2.
The boxes in a child's room come in all shapes and sizes and can be used in many ways. things.

Green, Rhonda Gowler. *When a Line Bends . . . a Shape Begins*. Illustrations by James Kaczman. Boston, Massachusetts: Houghton Mifflin Co., 1997. ISBN 0-395-78606-1.
Simple rhyming text and vibrant illustrations describe how shapes are formed from lines.

Seuss, Dr. *The Shape of Me and Other Stuff*. New York: Random House, Inc., 1973. ISBN 0-394-82687-6; 0-394-92687-0 (lib bdg).
Two children discuss the shapes that are all around them.

Colors and Shapes

Chester and Max Colors and Shapes Book. Illustrated by Jane Harvey. San Diego, California: Butterscotch Books, 1989. ISBN 0-934429-51-0.
With a little colorful paint, paper, and fabric, Chester and Max decorate all the shapes and sizes that they see.

RHYME AND RHYTHM ACTIVITIES

Read *Green Eggs and Ham* to the class and then make your own color treats. Discuss whether green eggs and ham are really different. Show students how a drop of blue food coloring mixed with eggs will make them green as you beat them for scrambled eggs. Let everyone try their hand at making their eggs green.

After sharing *Pink Drink* by S. Simeon and *Pink, Red, Blue, What Are You?* by Laura McGee Kvasnosky, have your students brainstorm a list of colorful rhymes. For example, the list might include red head and red shed or blue zoo and blue goo. Use the colorful phrases to create a color rhyme book for the class.

Try writing a poem using a color and some common objects following the step-by-step instructions on the activity sheet, "Writing a Poem, Step-by-Step."

Give each child a piece of white paper and a set of markers or crayons. As you read poems from *Hailstones and Halibut Bones* by Mary O'Neill, have the students draw what they hear in the poem. Concentrate on one color at a time, so students can focus on that color.

Plan a celebration of colors, spanning eight to twelve days or an entire month. Concentrate on one color each day (or whatever time period you want). Begin each day by sharing a color poem from *Hailstones and Halibut Bones* by Mary O'Neill or *Out of the Blue* by Hiawyn Oram. Set up a color table and have students bring in objects, materials, and even food for the color of the day. Include items to see, hear, smell, touch, and taste. Share color snacks each day. Some examples of color foods include the following:

Red: apples, strawberries, cherries, cranberry juice, cherry Jell-o, raspberries, tomato soup
Blue: blueberries, blue popcorn balls, blueberry muffins
Orange: cheese, carrots, oranges, orange juice, melon, orange sherbet
Yellow: pineapple, corn, bananas, lemonade, lemon Jell-o, egg salad, butter
White: popcorn balls, coconut, milk, cottage cheese, marshmallows, white bread
Brown: peanuts, pretzels, walnuts, hot chocolate, gingerbread, chocolate, graham crackers, wheat bread
Purple: grapes, plums, grape jelly, grape juice

Green: pickles, celery, broccoli, green beans, avocado, kiwi fruit, green peppers
Black: licorice, olives, raisins, Oreos, black jelly beans

Sponsor a similar celebration of shapes. Read shape poems, go on shape walks, and set up a shape table with things to see, hear, smell, touch, and taste. Share shape snacks every day. Some examples of shape foods include the following:

Circles: cored apples cut in circles, crackers, cucumber slices, Lifesavers, pizza, doughnut holes, cereal
Squares: crackers, ice cubes, bar cookies, cheese slices, sandwiches cut in fourths
Ovals: jelly beans, deviled eggs or hard-boiled eggs sliced lengthwise, grapes
Triangles: carrots, fancy finger sandwiches, crackers, pizza slices
Rectangles: gelatin cut in rectangles, granola bars, graham crackers, cheese and meat cut in rectangles
Stars: star fruit
Crescents or arcs: bananas, broken pretzels
Hearts: waffles and sandwiches cut with cookie cutters, cinnamon heart candies
(Use a cookie cutter or canape cutter or knife to cut sandwiches, bar cookies, meat, cheese, and gelatin into the desired shapes.)

Make posters with a blot of color in the center of each one. Pose a question, "What is _____?" and ask the children to name something of that color. After a few responses, read a line from Christina Rossetti's poem, *Colors*.

Share some of the color verses written by Hiawyn Oram in *Out of the Blue*. Use them to help make a list of familiar phrases or expressions that are associated with colors. Some examples include white elephant, beet red; feeling blue, mellow yellow. Have students research the phrases and locate information about their origin, history, and meaning.

Experiment with shape and/or color language. Make large-size charts in different shapes. Write shape language on the charts, and have students complete the phrases. For example, on a large circle, the children might complete the phrase, "Round as a _____," or on a square, the phrase

"Square as a _____." Use similar charts in different colors to complete phrases about colors.

A concrete or shape poem looks like the shape that it describes. Write a concrete poem about your favorite shape. Use the activity sheet, "Shape Poems," to help your students get a start with their own concrete poems.

Ask students to write a poem about shapes and things. Use the activity sheet, "Shapes and Things," to brainstorm ideas for the poem. Tell them to write the poem inside a silhouette of the shape.

Read the picture book rendition of the folk song, *Mary Wore Her Red Dress and Henry Wore His Green Sneakers*. Help students improvise their own verse, using the idea of clothing and colors or another theme such as daily events, familiar activities, or family. Substitute with the names of the children in your class.

Based on the pattern in Merle Peek's book, make a guessing game asking questions like "Who wore a pink hat?" or "Who got a new puppy?" Base the questions on the children in your class or group.

Have a party like Katy Bear's, complete with paper pink hats, cupcakes, and punch.

Writing a Poem Step-by Step

Write a poem about a favorite color, following the instructions below.

1. Choose a favorite color.

2. Make a list of some of the shades of the color.

3. Draw pictures of things that remind you of your favorite color. Think about the sounds, smells, tastes, feelings, and even dreams related to the color.

4. Using your color list and pictures for ideas, write a poem about your favorite color.

5. Give your poem a title.

A concrete or shape poem usually looks like the shape the word describes. Choose a shape and write a concrete poem about it. The example below may to help you get started.

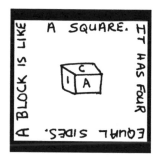

Shapes and Things

Think about some of your favorite things. Choose one of your favorite things and then list words in the chart below that describe or tell more about it. Use the list of descriptive words below to help you write a poem about your favorite object and its shape. Use a separate sheet of paper to draw a silhouette of the object and to write your poem.

My object is _____

Words That Describe My Favorite Object

Adjectives	Verbs	Nouns

5

SOCIAL STUDIES AND A WORLD OF COLORS AND SHAPES

Social studies involves a wide variety of activities, such as exploring the heritage of different groups of people, discovering faraway places, and examining various elements that affect society as a whole, such as transportation, holidays, and folktales. The number of social studies–related books using color and shape concepts is relatively small, but they are useful.

Chidi Only Likes Blue: An African Book of Colors, by Ifeoma Onyefulu, reveals how colors play a role in a Nigerian village. Young Chidi loves only the color blue, and his sister Nneka tries to teach about all the other colors. Nneka tells about other colors and why she loves them. Nneka talks about colors such as yellow, the color of the gari grains they eat; pink, the color of the flowers growing around their house; red, the color of Great-Uncle's special hat; gold, the color of mother's jewelry in the sun; and black from the uli trees, used to paint the houses. Despite her powerful words, Chidi still declares blue as his favorite color. Nneka's descriptions, along with the vivid, color photographs, provide a revealing look at Nigerian village life.

Kente Colors, by Debbi Chocolate, and *Hawaii Is a Rainbow,* by Stephanie Feeney, are two titles that deal directly with a particular culture. *Kente Colors* is a celebration of the beauty and tradition of the West African Kente cloth. The simple rhyming text describes the numerous ways that the Ashanti of Ghana and the Ewe of Ghana and Togo incorporate the fabric into their daily lives. The lush, vibrant illustrations are filled with deep blues, bright reds, rich purples, and warm yellows that almost leap off the page. Lavish illustrations convey the importance of the Kente cloth to the people of this region. Each color in Kente cloth symbolizes something. Ivory is for joy; green means a bountiful harvest; and blue symbolizes love. The author includes end-notes that describe the Kente patterns, the weaving process, and what the colors mean. While *Kente Colors* does deal with the topic of colors, it is a celebration of the cloth and how the colors reflect the history and culture of the region.

Stephanie Feeney celebrates a completely unrelated area of the world in her book, *Hawaii Is a Rainbow.* Feeney uses the colors of the rainbow as a way to organize pictures about the people, plants, and animals of this beautiful island. Most of the book is filled with color photographs of the island. The photographs focus on one color at a time, while showing the people, places, and things of Hawaii. The last third of the book includes explanatory notes about the photographs, detailing more information about the Hawaiian islands and the people, plants, and animals that inhabit them. Feeney's simple book is a colorful introduction to island life and to the fiftieth state of the Union.

Getting along with one another and looking at the differences in cultures is an important part of life. In *If We Were All the Same,* Fred Rogers takes a look at the issue of individuality and being different. While in the strictest sense, this is not a "color" book, colors are used throughout the story. Lady Elaine Fairchild is traveling in space and discovers a purple planet where everyone and everything is exactly the same. She likes it so much that when she returns home, she tries to get everyone to conform to one color and lifestyle. Her plan backfires when a purple bear and two purple people visit and decide they like the idea of different colors. They return home and soon the purple planet becomes a multicolored planet, where everyone lives in harmony. Mister Rogers provides a gentle message about being different and getting along with one another using the idea of colors as the basis of his story.

Margery Brown's Afro-Bet series features two titles on color that feature African-American children. In *Afro-Bets Book of Shapes,* Langston learns all about shapes as he makes cookies for his friends. Stef and Glo learn about primary and secondary colors in *Afro-Bets Book of Colors.* Both books are written especially for African Americans and are good examples of early concept books.

Folklore is an important part of cultural heritage and a useful tool for learning about other people. Three titles are particularly useful to show the role that color and shape have played in the folklore of different regions of the world. *Feathers Like a Rainbow: An Amazon Indian Tale,* by Flora, is a retelling of a South American Indian legend about birds and colors. The birds in the rain forest decide to steal colors from the hummingbird to make their own feathers more beautiful. Things don't exactly work out the way the birds plan, when only one or two colors stick with each bird. Rich, intense paintings of the lush Amazon rain forest fill the pages of this vibrant tale of birds and colors. In the Asian tale, *How the World Got Its Color,* Marilyn Hirsch tells of a time when there were no colors except those in a set of paints given to an artist by the gods. While her father is away, Miki borrows the paints and begins to fill the world with color. When her father returns home, he is very angry until the gods agree with Miki that the world is better filled with color. The illustrations start out in black-and-white ink sketches, but soon colors fill the pages as Miki begins painting.

In yet another region of the world, Ann Grifalconi's *The Village of Round and Square Houses* relates an African legend about the remote village of Tos, a village that actually exists in the hills of central Africa. In Tos the women live in round houses, and men live in square ones. According to the legend, when the volcanic mountain Naka erupted, the villagers were forced to flee for their lives. When the volcano quieted down and they returned, the villagers were covered with gray ash and unrecognizable. Only two houses remained in the village, a square one and a round one. The chief wanted to rebuild the village immediately, so he instructed the tall gray shapes to live in the square house and do the work in the field. The round gray ones were to live in the round house. Ever since that day, the women have lived in the round houses, while the men stay in the square houses. Since Grifalconi has

actually visited Tos, her illustrations contribute to the reader's understanding of this different way of life. Grifalconi blends fiction, anthropology, and folklore in her tale of life in Tos.

Hannah Giffard has written a very simple but colorful board book, *Red Bus,* about different modes of transportation. Each page contains a very simple drawing of the vehicle along with an identification of it (red bus, blue train, yellow helicopter, and more). In *Catch the Red Bus!* by Julia Killingback, a group of busy bears go on a trip. They try a variety of colorful vehicles, including a yellow cart and a purple plane, to reach their destination. Bruce McMillan concentrates on shapes found on one type of transportation in *Fire Engine Shapes.* A small child goes exploring and, in the process, reveals all the geometric shapes that make a fire engine. The full-color photographs in this unique book show different parts of the fire engine and how they represent variety of shapes. The main body of the book contains no text, but notes in the back show the seven shapes found in the photographs. McMillan also includes notes about the child in the photographs, the fire engine, the camera, film, and time of the photographs.

Shapes and holidays seem to go hand in hand in Frank Daniel's Fun Shapes series of board books as well as *Christmas Shapes* from Covent Garden Books' Snapshot series. Daniel focuses on one single shape in each of his four holiday books. *Christmas* shows how the lively season is filled not only with joy but with circles. A die-cut of a shape is cut through the board book from cover to cover. As the reader turns each page, the circle becomes a part of something associated with the holiday season. Circles make up Santa's glasses as he reads a long list, the heads of snowmen and snowballs flying through the air are circles, even the wheels of toy cars and the eyes of dolls are circles. In *Halloween,* Daniel concentrates on triangles associated with this season. Pumpkin eyes, witch hats, and even spaces between skeleton bones are triangles. *Chanukah* concentrates on the Jewish holiday and all the squares associated with it, such as dreidels, spinning toys played with during this time. *Thanksgiving* focuses on semicircles. All four of these books adequately introduce both simple shapes and holidays. The Snapshot shape book concentrates on all kinds of shapes found during the Christmas season in *Christmas Shapes.* This tiny board book includes color photographs against a stark white background. The book displays nine basic shapes: colorful ornaments for circles, cookies for hearts, and decorated trees for triangles, for example. No identification of the shape appears on the page with the item, but a double-page spread in the back identifies each Christmas-related shape.

If You Want to Find Golden, by Eileen Spinelli, is an excellent book for discussing colors and exploring city life. The colors of the city are revealed through imaginative verses and rich, vivid illustrations. The longer text and detailed descriptions make Spinelli's book a better choice for older students (middle grades and up). Every verse begins with the phrase "If you want to find . . ." followed by the name of a color and a detailed description of several objects in that color typically found in a city scene. For example, with the color brown, Spinelli describes the weeds growing through cracks in the sidewalks and a teddy bear in a shop window. To introduce the color green, a local grocer shows his wide array of green goods: onions, lettuce, spinach, and cilantro.

Color and shape books dealing with social studies are useful tools for discussing people and culture. Folktales offer the reader a look at the past, whereas other books show how important colors and shapes are in the present. By using colors and shapes as a tool to hook readers, we can offer them a better understanding of their own culture and heritage as well as those of others.

BIBLIOGRAPHY

Colors

Brown, Margery W. *Afro-Bets Book of Colors*. Illustrated by Culverson Blair. Orange, New Jersey: Just Us Books, Inc., 1991. ISBN 0-940975-28-9.
Stef and Glo learn all about colors and how they are used.

Chocolate, Debbi. *Kente Colors*. Illustrated by John Ward. New York: Walker and Company, 1996. ISBN 0-8027-8389-9 (lib bdg); 0-8027-8388-0.
This joyful ode to Kente cloth celebrates the beauty and tradition of this West African fabric.

Feeney, Stephanie. *Hawaii Is a Rainbow*. Photographs by Jeff Reese. Honolulu, Hawaii: University of Hawaii Press, 1985. ISBN 0-8248-1007-4.
The colors of the rainbow organize this collection of photographs about the people, places, and things of Hawaii.

Flora. *Feathers Like a Rainbow: An Amazon Indian Tale*. New York: Harper & Row Publishers, 1989. ISBN 0-06-021837-1; 0-06-021838-X (lib. bdg).
Tired of their dark feathers, the birds in the rain forest decide to steal colors from the hummingbird.

Giffard, Hannah. *Red Bus*. New York: Tambourine Books, 1993. ISBN 0-688-12443-7.
Modes of transportation introduce colors.

Hirsch, Marilyn. *How the World Got Its Color*. New York: Crown Publishers, Inc., 1972.
Miki borrows her father's paints and begins to brighten up a colorless world.

Killingback, Julia. *Catch the Red Bus!* New York: William Morrow & Co., 1985. ISBN 0-688-05783-7.
A red bus and a green train are only two of the vehicles that the busy bears use on their trip.

Onyefulu, Ifeoma. *Chidi Only Likes Blue: An African Book of Colors*. New York: Cobblehill Books, 1997. ISBN 0-525-65243-4.
Despite powerful words from his sister Nneka about the colors of the village, Chidi still chooses blue as his favorite color.

Rogers, Fred. *If We Were All the Same*. Illustrated by Pat Sustendal. New York: Random House, 1987. ISBN 0-394-88778-6; 0-394-98778-0 (lib bdg).
The people of the purple planet decide to become more colorful when they discover that other worlds are not the same as theirs.

Spinelli, Eileen. *If You Want to Find Golden*. Paintings by Stacey Schuett. Morton Grove, Illinois: Albert Whitman and Company, 1993. ISBN 0-8075-3585-0.
Imaginative verse and rich, vivid illustrations reveal the colors of the city.

Shapes

Brown, Margery W. *Afro-Bets Book of Shapes*. Illustrated by Culverson Blair. Orange, New Jersey: Just Us Books, Inc., 1991. ISBN 0-940975-29-7.
As he makes cookies for all his friends, Langston learns about shapes.

Christmas Shapes. New York: Covent Garden Books, 1994. ISBN 1-56458-822-X.
From twinkling stars to rings of holly, the shapes of Christmas come alive in this tiny board book.

Daniel, Frank. *Chanukah*. New York: Macmillan Publishing Co., 1993. ISBN 0-689-71733.
Squares and Chanukah are the subject of this Jewish holiday board book.

Daniel, Frank. *Christmas*. New York: Macmillan Publishing Co., 1993. ISBN 0-689-71734-2.
Christmas introduces circles in this board book.

Daniel, Frank. *Halloween*. New York: Macmillan Publishing Co., 1993. ISBN 0-689-71736-9.
Pumpkins, skeletons, and witches shape up with triangles in a special holiday book.

Daniel, Frank. *Thanksgiving*. New York: Macmillan Publishing Co., 1993. ISBN 0-689-71735-0.
Semicircles and Thanksgiving have much in common in this American holiday board book.

Grifalconi, Ann. *The Village of Round and Square Houses*. Boston, Massachusetts: Little, Brown and Company, 1986. ISBN 0-316-32862-6.
A blend of fiction, anthropology, and folklore center around the remote African village of Tos.

McMillan, Bruce. *Fire Engine Shapes*. New York: Lothrop, Lee and Shepard, 1988. ISBN 0-688-07842-7; 0-688-07843-5 (lib bdg).
A close examination of a fire engine reveals the many shapes that make up its sleek design.

SOCIAL STUDIES ACTIVITIES

Read and discuss Kente cloth using *Kente Colors* by Debbi Chocolate. Talk about the symbolism of the different colors and patterns used in this traditional fabric of Ghana. Have students design their own Kente pattern using a variety of colors.

After sharing Fred Rogers's *If We Were All the Same,* discuss the importance of being different and the issues of individuality. Emphasize how being different is what makes the world wonderful and interesting.

Read *The Village of Round and Square Houses,* by Ann Grifalconi, then briefly discuss the cultural practice of men and women living separately. Talk about round and square designs. Divide the class into small groups and ask each group to make a model of a round or square house. Decide what materials are necessary and how each group will build its house. Make round furniture for the round house and square furniture for the square house. As an alternative, have students draw round and square houses and then draw or cut out pictures of round and square furniture.

Discuss how families live in all different kinds of homes. Talk about some of the different types of housing, including apartments, one-family homes, two-family homes, mobile homes, houseboats, tents, and igloos. Ask the children to talk about their home. Then distribute the activity sheet, "Home, Sweet Home." Provide a variety of different paper shapes in a variety of colors and sizes. Have the children glue the different shapes on the activity sheet to create a collage picture of their home. Encourage them to add details, such as people, trees, fences, and flowers, using markers, crayons, or other writing tools.

Give each student the word puzzle sheet, "Colorful Vehicles," to find the different modes of colorful transportation based on the board book *Red Bus,* by Hannah Giffard, and *Catch the Red Bus!* by Julia Killingback.

Using the Fun Shapes series by Frank Daniel as a model, ask students to create their own die-cut holiday shape book. Have each small group choose a holiday and a shape as the focus of the book. Each group writes a brief story about the shape and things associated with the holiday while other students work on the shape illustrations. For example, they may combine an oval with Easter, incorporating oval eggs and bunny ears as part of the tale.

Following the pattern set up in *Christmas Shapes,* use another holiday and write a simple explanation of the shapes associated with it. Take photographs or draw pictures of the different shapes. For example, a shape book on Halloween might include a harvest moon for a circle, a witches hat for a triangle, and trick-or-treat bags for rectangles. Use this project with older students by having them create a board book for preschoolers.

After sharing *If You Want to Find Golden,* by Eileen Spinelli, discuss the verse and city scenes within the book. Have students brainstorm city themes and write their own color verses describing a city scene. Some ideas for different themes might include a bus station, zoo, sidewalk vendor, park, or storefront scene.

Glue the different shapes to create a collage picture of your home. Add details such as people, flowers, and trees with markers or crayons after your picture dries.

Colorful Vehicles

Colorful vehicles are used in *Catch the Red Bus!* by Julie Killingback and *Red Bus* by Hannah Giffard. See if you can find the colorful vehicles listed below in this mixed-up word puzzle. Circle the vehicles as you find them. They can be found up and down, across, or diagonally and spelled either forward or backward.

WHITE BOAT   BLACK CAR   BLUE CAR
YELLOW HELICOPTER   ORANGE BIKE   PURPLE PLANE
BLACK TAXI   GREEN TRAIN   GREEN BOAT
PINK BICYCLE   YELLOW CART   GRAY SUBMARINE
BLUE TRAIN   WHITE AIRPLANE   ORANGE TRUCK
PURPLE BALLOON   RED BUS

```
Y E L L O W C A R T G W I
E E U K R H M L R W R H P
L B B L A C K C A R A I P
L O O A N K M I K M Y T U
O R A N G E B I K E S E R
W G R E E N B O A T U A P
H K L M T P N O D C B I L
E B X Q R B O W I M M R E
L C B L U E C A R H A P P
I B L A C K T A X I R L L
C H N V K P S D C V I A A
O Y T R E D B U S H N N N
P I N K B I C Y C L E E E
T Y N D T A O B E T I H W
E E B L U E T R A I N Y T
R G R E E N T R A I N H J
P U R P L E B A L L O O N
```

6

EXPLORING SCIENCE AND MATH WITH COLORS AND SHAPES

From the moment of birth, a child explores the world around her or him. Faces, people, nature, and even colors and shapes help the child examine, explore, and experiment with things in the world around him. Many of the books that emphasize colors and shapes help children to learn about animals, plants, and nature and discover their connection between colors, shapes, and numbers. Animals were discussed in chapter 3, so this chapter concentrates on nature and science along with the connections among math, science, and shapes. These books serve as supplementary resources to the science and math curriculums.

From the purely scientific angle, two series discuss in detail how colors are made, how we see colors, and the role color plays in our daily lives. Both Barbara J. Behm (The Science of Color series) and Gabrielle Woolfitt (Colors series) concentrate on facts about a color and then use photographs to show things in the featured color. Barbara Behm takes a look at the purpose and effect of color in her series. In *Investigating the Color Red,* the reader learns about the rich vibrant world of red and its importance to life: red stoplights, flowers, sunsets, lipstick, fruit, and even blood. In *Green,* Woolfitt focuses on green places, green animals, green foods, and green projects. The pages are filled with color photographs along with brief paragraphs describing the subjects. Each series has four books featuring one color (red, blue, green, and yellow). This scientific treatment makes both series useful with younger students in identifying colors and with older students for more detailed instruction on the role of colors.

Sally Morgan's series, The World of Shapes, deals with different shapes in a more scientific and mathematical context. In *Circles and Spheres,* soap bubbles, dinner plates, grapes, and wheels are only a few of the familiar objects that demonstrate the concept of round objects. Bright, vibrant colors border each double-page spread, and color photographs of the objects fill the pages. A variety of projects, such as measuring circumference, making a spinning top, and locating circles and spheres in everyday situations, are included in each of the four titles in the series. This informative series would supplement a math unit on geometric shapes well.

Color in nature is the topic of a board book series from the National Geographic Society. Each of the six books focuses on a color found in nature. The books are wordless with only a simple scene used to introduce the color. In *Red* a small red bird flies away, returns with a worm to its nest in a cherry tree, and finally meets a ladybug just as a baby red bird pops out of the nest. *Blue* takes a look at ocean life, where a crab scuttles across the seafloor, meets a shell that opens its eyes, then scurries away when a big blue fish swims by. Each of the four double-page spreads in these six books is filled with attractive drawings of objects in the featured color.

Shapes in nature is the topic of *Shapes in Nature,* by Judy Feldman, and *Listen to a Shape,* by Marcia Brown. Feldman uses color photographs to show natural shapes such as a heart shape found in the leaves of a violet wood sorrel. The only text in the book is notes telling about the photograph and photographer. The photographs are clear and sharp, offering the reader an entirely different way to look at shapes. Marcia Brown also uses color photographs of nature in *Listen to a Shape.* She shows how circles, squares, crescents, and other shapes are found in trees, swans, fish, and water. The poetic captions used throughout the book are written in free-verse style and encourage the reader to be more aware of the environment. Both of these books would help to sharpen a child's observation skills.

Tana Hoban has a unique way of seeing the extraordinary in familiar things, and she has written four titles that take a look at shapes in our everyday surroundings. In *Shapes, Shapes, Shapes,* Hoban uses color photographs to show how rounded and angular shapes can be found everywhere. At the beginning of the book, Hoban tells the readers to look for certain shapes as they read the book. Each page is a photograph of an ordinary scene, such as a small boy sailing a boat, a cluster of hanging baskets, and a stack of boxes. While simple shapes are certainly central to the book, Hoban also shows lots of arcs, hexagons, parallelograms, trapezoids, and other unusual shapes. Circular objects in the everyday world are the focus of *Round & Round & Round.* Hoban uses virtually no text and color photographs to show the many round things that surround us. Wheels and seals, peas and hoops, bubbles and beads are among them. In *Spirals, Curves, Fanshapes, and Lines,* Hoban again uses virtually no text to accompany her color photographs of some intriguing shapes. All three of Hoban's titles encourage readers to sharpen their perceptions about objects and to nurture an appreciation of ordinary objects.

Several books introduce geometric shapes to children. In *Three Sides and the Round One,* Margaret Friskey uses a simple story to introduce basic geometric shapes. A circle and a triangle get together and discuss the basic geometric shapes they see in everyday objects. Friskey gives many examples of spheres, cones, cubes, and other shapes. Ivan Bulloch shows how to put shapes into action in *Shapes.* By applying math to "real" life, Bulloch invites the reader to participate in this how-to math book as he shows how the world is made up of basic shapes. He suggests activites such as making a desk organizer and jewelry, to show how shapes are important. Fulvio Testa uses familiar things to introduce some abstract concepts in *If You Look around You.* One simple sentence describes the action and shape that can be seen on the facing page. In one scene, children on a bridge throw stones in the water, while the text describes how circles form when a stone drops in water.

In yet another book from Dorling Kindersley, Lydia Sharman tackles *The Amazing Book of Shapes.* This oversized volume uses stark white backgrounds with vibrant photographs of real objects and colorful paper designs to explore math through shapes and patterns. Each section clearly describes shapes or a mathematical concept involving shapes and patterns. Each new concept is supported with a craft activity accompanied by step-by-step photographs and clear, concise instructions. In addition, the book includes a mirror bookmark for exploring symmetry, a foldout section with shape stencils to help draw accurate circles, triangles, and squares, and pattern grids to use for designing detailed geometric patterns. *The Amazing Book of Shapes* could be used with primary students, but for the most part, the concepts and information would be more useful with upper elementary and even high school students.

Colors and plants are the topic of four books that would be useful with preschoolers and older elementary students. *Growing Colors* by Bruce McMillan and *Planting a Rainbow* by Lois Ehlert are picture books that show all the colors found in common flowers, fruits, and vegetables. McMillan uses color photographs of garden vegetables and orchard fruits to show color in nature. Each double page includes a photograph showing the object from the distance with the facing page a close-up photograph of the same object. For the color red, McMillan shows red raspberries on a bush, while the facing page is a close-up photograph of five of the red raspberries on the bush. Beautiful photographs of all kinds of familiar foods, such as orange carrots, yellow squash, blue grapes, white onions, and purple plums are used throughout the book to introduce colors and to show how important colors are in nature. In *Planting a Rainbow* a small child and a mother plant bulbs, seeds, and plants in their special garden. Ehlert uses bold, vibrant colors throughout the book to show how the flowers form a color rainbow. The text is very simple, consisting of only the names of the colors and flowers. Bulbs, seeds, and plants fill the garden with a rainbow of colors.

Two nonfiction titles, *Roses Red, Violets Blue: Why Flowers Have Colors* by Sylvia A. Johnson and *Blue Potatoes, Orange Tomatoes* by Rosalind Creasy, complete a study of colors and plants. Johnson takes a serious, detailed look at the nature and function of flower colors in *Roses Red, Violets Blue* and their role in attracting animal pollinators. The beautiful color photographs include a unique look at "ultraviolet" colors of flowers not visible to the human eye. *Blue Potatoes, Orange Tomatoes* looks at colorful vegetables that anyone can grow. Although the emphasis is on gardening rather than colors, Creasy presents a colorful cornucopia of common vegetables in the second half of the book. The first half provides guidelines for planning the garden, preparing soil, feeding, watering, weeding, and controlling insect pests. In the second half, the reader receives detailed instructions in growing a colorful array of eight common vegetables, including blue potatoes, red chard, purple string beans, and multicolored radishes. For each vegetable, the information includes varieties, planting and harvesting instructions, and even a recipe for cooking the vegetable. With vivid illustrations by Ruth Heller and a plethora of information by Creasy, this book will get any would-be gardener started on the road to colorful organic gardening.

Several books present colors and shapes in the animal kingdom. In *A Color of His Own* by Leo Lionni, a chameleon goes on a search for his own color and in the process finds a true friend. When the chameleon moves from one place to another, it changes colors from green to yellow to red to black or whatever object it is sitting on. Although the camouflage may come in handy when enemies are near, the chameleon wants a color of his own. In a search for his identity, he discovers friendship and happiness. Lionni has written a simple story about color and how the chameleon changes his color. Other animals also use changing colors to protect themselves. Some fact books that give detailed information about such animals are listed in the chapter bibliography.

Creatures in the sea can be found in all colors and sizes in three books. In the board book, *The Sea's Many Colors* by Elaine Lonergan, the reader sees the wonders of the sea and their colors when baby Shamu introduces a red lobster, a green buoy, an orange pelican beak, and himself, baby black Shamu. This cute cartoonish book is suitable for preschoolers. *Ocean Parade: A Counting Book* by Patricia MacCarthy concentrates on counting the creatures that cross the pages as it combines color concepts with number concepts. From twenty green sea horses to thirty little purple fish, the reader enjoys brilliant colors in the silk batik paintings. Photographs and vivid languages are used to introduce the colors of marine life in *Rainbows of the Sea* by Meredith Thomas. It is only at a second glance that the reader finds that the photographs contain paper sculptures instead of real marine animals and plants. The paper sculptures were photographed

with special lighting and focusing to give the impression of being underwater. Sky blue soldier crabs, cobalt-patterned angelfish, dainty rose anemones, and buttery little lemon fish are only a few of the colorful creatures of the sea featured in this book. Marine animals are the subject of Suse McDonald's *Sea Shapes*. Each double-page spread shows how a shape is transformed into a sea animal. On the left a series of three blocks introduces the shape and shows how it transforms into a familiar sea animal. A circle becomes part of a whale; a hexagon becomes part of a turtle shell; and an oval becomes part of an octopus. The right facing page shows the sea creature in an undersea collage scene. In the back of the book, McDonald includes brief facts about each of the marine animals shown. The collage illustrations make *Sea Shapes* a remarkable introduction to the world of geometric shapes.

In *White Is the Moon,* Valerie Greeley easily explores concepts of color, day and night, and the natural world all rolled up in one simple story. This circular tale takes the reader through night and day as the moon or sun moves across the sky. Each double-page spread follows the same pattern with a lyrical four-line verse on the left-hand page, which is framed in the featured color. A drawing of an object appears above the verse, and the object appears in a natural scene on the facing page. Each verse builds on the previous one because the animal that ends the previous verse is featured in the next verse. The illustrations are beautiful and so realistic that the animals look alive. While some might call *White Is the Moon* a bedtime story, it is a lovely read-aloud tale of nature and colors. *Colors* by Heidi Groennel compares nature and colors, but everything is from a child's point of view. The illustrations are filled with bright, cheerful colors accompanied by simple sentences that compare two unrelated things. While actual colors are never mentioned, the unexpected comparisons open the door to some lively discussions and opportunities to compare even more colors. From an elephant the color of a rainy day to an inchworm the color of grass, Groennel's book is an interesting approach to the concept of colors.

One of the best books to use when talking about shapes is *The Greedy Triangle* by Marilyn Burns. A triangle tires of having only three sides, so he asks the shapeshifter to change him. First, he turns into a quadrilateral, then a pentagon, a hexagon, and other shapes, until the triangle's friends no longer recognize him. This clever story shows how shapes are everywhere—part of a computer screen, a floor tile, or a section of a ball. The acrylic-and-colored-pencil illustrations have bright colors, abstract designs, and smiling shapes. Two pages in the back serve as a guide to parents on using the book to reinforce math lessons.

Many color and shape books that deal with science and math subjects may supplement the curriculum at primary through high school levels. At the lower levels, they serve as simple stories or informational books about colors and shapes found in natural surroundings. With older students, they may serve as a springboard for further research, as models of relationships in nature, and as references about plants, animals, and the environment.

Colors

Ardley, Neil. *The Science Book of Color*. San Diego, California: Harcourt Brace Jovanovich, 1991. ISBN 0-15-200576-5.

Ardley explains the principles of color and gives instructions for a variety of simple experiments.

Behm, Barbara J. *Investigating the Color Blue*. Milwaukee, Wisconsin: Gareth Stevens Publishing Co., 1993. ISBN 0-8368-1028-7.

Dyes, gems, feathers, and eyes are examples of the calm and cool world of blue.

Behm, Barbara J. *Investigating the Color Green*. Milwaukee, Wisconsin: Gareth Stevens Publishing Co., 1993. ISBN 0-8368-1029-5.

The color green appears in plants, gemstones, animals, and more.

Behm, Barbara J. *Investigating the Color Red*. Milwaukee, Wisconsin: Gareth Stevens Publishing Co., 1993. ISBN 0-8368-1027-9.

From red flowers and fruit to blood and poor health, the reader learns all about the color red and where it appears in our world.

Behm, Barbara J. *Investigating the Color Yellow*. Milwaukee, Wisconsin: Gareth Stevens Publishing Co., 1993. ISBN 0-8368-1030-9.

This title explores the bright and sunny world of yellow and how it fits into everyday life.

Blue. Washington, D.C.: National Geographic Society, 1990.

Wordless text and photographs of a colorful undersea world introduce the color blue in this small board book.

Coldrey, Jennifer, and Karen Goldie-Morrison, eds. *Danger Colors*. New York: G. P. Putnam, 1986. ISBN 0-399-21341-4.

This fact book describes characteristics of a variety of animals whose color protects them from their enemies.

Coldrey, Jennifer, and Karen Goldie-Morrison, eds. *Hide and Seek*. New York: G. P. Putnam's Sons, 1986. ISBN 0-399-21342-2.

Animals with permanent or intermittent camouflage capabilities aid in preying and protecting themselves.

Creasy, Rosalind. *Blue Potatoes, Orange Tomatoes*. Illustrated by Ruth Heller. San Francisco, California: Sierra Club Books for Children, 1994. ISBN 0-87156-576-5.

The reader learns of the joys of organic gardening and the surprises of a rainbow crop.

Ehlert, Lois. *Planting a Rainbow*. San Diego, California: Harcourt Brace Jovanovich, 1988. ISBN 0-15-262609-3.

A child and a mother plant a rainbow of flowers in their garden.

Green. Washington, D.C.: National Geographic Society, 1990.

A small green frog and his pond friends introduce the color green.

Greeley, Valerie. *White Is the Moon*. New York: Macmillan Publishing Co., 1991. ISBN 0-02-736915-3.

From night to day and back to night, these short poems introduce colors and animals.

Groennel, Heidi. *Colors*. Boston, Massachusetts: Little, Brown and Company, 1990. ISBN 0-316-31843-4.

Comparisons between things in a child's world and things in nature take the reader through a world of color.

Johnson, Sylvia A. *Roses Red, Violets Blue: Why Flowers Have Color*. Photographs by Yuko Sato. Minneapolis, Minnesota: Lerner, 1991. ISBN 0-8225-1594-6.

Johnson presents an unusual look at the nature and function of flower colors.

Kalman, Bobbie. *The Colors of Nature*. New York: Crabtree Publishing Company, 1993. ISBN 0-86505-557-2 (lib bdg); 0-86505-583-1 (pbk).

Facts and activites help students explore the role that color plays in the lives of plants, animals, and people.

Lionni, Leo. *A Color of His Own*. New York: Alfred A. Knopf, 1975. ISBN 0-679-84197-0; 0-679-94197-5 (lib bdg).

When a chameleon searches for a color of his own, he discovers happiness and a true friend.

Lonergan, Elaine. *The Sea's Many Colors*. Illustrated by Paul Lopez. Bridgeport, Connecticut: Third Story Books, 1994. ISBN 1-884506-01-1.

Baby Shamu introduces the colors of the ocean.

MacCarthy, Patricia. *Ocean Parade: A Counting Book*. New York: Dial Books, 1990. ISBN 0-8037-0780-0.

A swarm of colorful fish swim through the paintings in this unusual counting book.

McMillan, Bruce. *Growing Colors*. New York: Lothrop, Lee and Shepard Books, 1988. ISBN 0-688-07844-3; 0-688-07845-1 (lib bdg).

Photographs of garden vegetables and orchard fruits show colors as they grow in nature.

Milburn, Constance. *Let's Look at Colors*. New York: The Bookwright Press, 1988. ISBN 0-531-18205-3.

Simple text and illustrations encourage children to look at colors in the world around them.

Orange. Washington, D.C.: National Geographic Society, 1990.

An orange pumpkin starts the parade of orange things in this board book.

Purple. Washington, D.C.: National Geographic Society, 1990.

A butterfly, a snail, and a snake introduce the color purple.

Red. Washington, D.C.: National Geographic Society, 1990.

A little red bird feeds its baby in this simple tale.

Reich, Janet. *Gus and the Green Thing*. New York: Walker and Company, 1993. ISBN 0-8027-8252-3; 0-8027-8253-1 (lib bdg).

Unhappy with living a gray life in the gray city, Gus encounters a green thing that shows him a world of life and growth.

Rockwell, Anne. *Willy Can Count*. New York: Arcade Publishing, 1989. ISBN 1-55970-013-0.

As Willy and his mother go for a stroll, he counts a variety of colorful items.

Stockdale, Susan. *Nature's Paintbrush: The Patterns and Colors around You*. New York: Simon and Schuster, 1999. ISBN 0-689-81081-4

From flower petals to a toucan's bill, children are introduced to the colors of the animals and plants of the rain forest.

Thomas, Meredith. *Rainbows of the Sea*. Photographs by Adrian Lander. Greenvale, New York: MONDO Publishing, 1998. ISBN 1-57255-432-0; 0-57255-431-5 (pbk).

Striking paper sculptures of marine life are used to introduce colors.

Woolfitt, Gabrielle. *Blue*. Minneapolis, Minnesota: Carolrhoda Books, Inc., 1991. ISBN 0-87614-704-X (lib bdg).

Flowers, clothes, water, gems, and more help the reader examine the color blue.

Woolfitt, Gabrielle. *Green*. Minneapolis, Minnesota: Carolrhoda Books, Inc., 1992. ISBN 0-87614-705-8.

Herbs, fruits, parrots, and leaves help the reader examine the color green.

Woolfitt, Gabrielle. *Red*. Minneapolis, Minnesota: Carolrhoda Books, 1992. ISBN 0-87614-706-6.

Red foods, animals, flowers, and even festivals help the reader examine the color red.

Woolfitt, Gabrielle. *Yellow*. Minneapolis, Minnesota: Carolrhoda Books, 1991. ISBN 0-87614-707-4 (lib bdg).

Short paragraphs and color photographs of yellow objects help the reader examine the color yellow.

Wright, Rachel. *Look at Color and Camouflage*. New York: Franklin Watts, 1988. ISBN 0-531-14000-8.

The reader learns about a variety of animals who use color to hide and protect themselves.

Yellow. Washington, D.C.: National Geographic Society, 1990.

As the sun rises, all kinds of yellow things come alive in the pages of this board book.

Shapes

Allington, Richard L. *Shapes*. Illustrated by Lois Ehlert. Milwaukee, Wisconsin: Raintree Publishers, Inc., 1979. ISBN 0-8172-1277-9 (lib bdg).

This informative book introduces twenty different geometric shapes.

Audry-Iljic, Francoise, and Thierry Courtin. *Discover Shapes*. Hauppauge, New York: Barron's Educational Series, Inc., 1994. ISBN 0-8120-6499-2.

From point to line and area to volume, this book explores basic geometric shapes.

Axelrod, Amy. *Pigs on the Ball: Fun with Math and Sports*. Pictures by Sharon McGinley-Nally. New York: Simon and Schuster, 1998. ISBN 0-689-81565-4.

When the Pig family visits a miniature golf course, they learn all about shapes.

Brown, Marcia. *Listen to a Shape*. New York: Franklin Watts, 1979. ISBN 0-531-02383-4; 0-531-02930-1 (lib bdg).

Circles, squares, crescents, and other shapes are shown as they appear in nature.

Bulloch, Ivan. *Shapes*. New York: Thomson Learning, 1994. ISBN 1-56847-232-3.

This book not only introduces basic shapes, but also offers many activities to put the shapes into action.

Burns, Marilyn. *The Greedy Triangle*. Illustrated by Gordon Silveria. New York: Scholastic, Inc., 1994. ISBN 0-590-48991-7.

When the triangle tires of his shape, he asks the shapeshifter for some help and added lines.

Carle, Eric. *My Very First Book of Shapes*. New York: HarperCollins, 1974. ISBN 0-694-00013-2.

The reader matches the correct shape with an illustration on the bottom half of the page.

Crews, Donald. *Ten Black Dots*. New York: Greenwillow Books, 1968, 1986. ISBN 0-688-06067-6; 0-688-06068-4 (pbk).

This counting book takes a look at all the things one can do with ten black dots.

Feldman, Judy. *Shapes in Nature*. Chicago: Illinois: Childrens Press, 1991. ISBN 0-516-05102-4.
Photographs show how different shapes exist all around us.

Fisher, Leonard Everett. *Look Around! A Book about Shapes*. New York: Viking Kestrel, 1987. ISBN 0-670-80869-5.
Three-dimensional colorful pictures present shapes in familiar scenes.

Friskey, Margaret. *Three Sides and the Round One*. Chicago, Illinois: Childrens Press, 1973. ISBN 0-516-03627-0.
When a circle and a triangle get together, they discuss some basic geometric shapes.

Grover, Max. *Circles and Squares Everywhere!* San Diego, California: Browndeer Press/Harcourt Brace, 1996. ISBN 0-15-200091-7.
Tires, trucks, windows, boats, houses: circles and squares are everywhere.

Hoban, Tana. *Round & Round & Round*. New York: Greenwillow Books, 1986. ISBN 0-688-01813-0; 0-688-01814-9 (lib bdg).
Photographs of balloons, bubbles, and beads illustrate what is round.

Hoban, Tana. *Shapes, Shapes, Shapes*. New York: Greenwillow Books, 1986. ISBN 0-688-05832-9; 0-688-05833-7 (lib bdg).
Rounded and angular shapes appear all around us.

Hoban, Tana. *Spirals, Curves, Fanshapes, and Lines*. New York: Greenwillow Books, 1992. ISBN 0-688-11228-5; 0-688-11229-3 (lib bdg).
Familiar objects come in intriguing shapes.

Kightley, Rosalinda. *Shapes*. Boston, Massachusetts: Little, Brown & Company, 1986. ISBN 0-316-54005-6.
Shapes of all sorts help people construct everyday objects.

McDonald, Suse. *Sea Shapes*. Orlando, Florida: Harcourt, Brace & Co., 1994. ISBN 0-15-200027-5.
In this undersea world, shapes transform themselves into all kinds of sea creatures.

Morgan, Sally. *Circles and Spheres*. New York: Thomson Learning, 1994. ISBN 1-56847-235-8.
Soap bubbles, plates, and grapes are a few of the round things found in this informative book.

Morgan, Sally. *Spirals*. New York: Thomson Learning, 1994. ISBN 1-56847-278-1.
Spirals of all kinds are found in this title.

Morgan, Sally. *Squares and Cubes*. New York: Thomson Learning, 1994. ISBN 1-56847-234-X.
An avalanche of squares and cubes includes ice cubes, street signs, and TV sets.

Morgan, Sally. *Triangles and Pyramids*. New York: Thomson Learning, 1994. ISBN 1-56847-277-3.
All sorts of familiar objects form triangles.

Murphy, Stuart J. *Circus Shapes*. Illustrated by Edward Miller. New York: HarperCollins, 1997. ISBN 0-06-027437-9 (lib bdg); 0-06-446713-9 (pbk).
The reader searches for shapes at the circus.

Pluckrose, Henry. *Shapes*. Chicago, Illinois: Childrens Press, 1994. ISBN 0-516-05456-2.
Colorful photographs of familiar things introduce basic shapes.

Schlein, Miriam. *Shapes*. Pictures by Sam Berman. New York: William R. Scott, Inc., 1952.
Round and square objects are featured.

Schroeder, P., and J. Donisch. *Shapes*. Vero Beach, Florida: Rourke Publishing Group, 1996. ISBN 0-86625-577-X.
Rhyming text accompanies color photographs that introduce basic geometric shapes.

The Shapes Book. Encyclopedia Britannica, Inc., 1974. ISBN 0-85229-298-8.
This fact book discusses shapes and shows some very special examples.

Sharman, Lydia. *The Amazing Book of Shapes: Explore Math through Shapes and Patterns*. New York: Dorling Kindersley, 1994. ISBN 1-56458-514-X.
The reader explores shapes and patterns through a variety of creative projects.

Testa, Fulvio. *If You Look around You*. New York: Dial Books for Young Readers, 1983. ISBN 0-8037-003-2.
Scenes of children playing introduce geometric shapes.

Thoburn, Tina. *Discovering Shapes*. Pictures by James Caraway. New York: Western Publishing Co., 1963, 1970.
Everything you always wanted to know about shapes, shapes, and more shapes.

SCIENCE AND MATH ACTIVITIES

Read *The Science Book of Color,* by Neil Ardley, and try some of its experiments with older students. "Invisible Ink" is sure to be popular.

Share books from the colors series by Barbara J. Behm and Gabrielle Woolfitt. Discuss how both authors chose a color and conducted a thorough investigation on the role that the color plays in our world. Divide the class into small groups of two to three. Each group chooses a color (other than the four in the series) and conducts its own investigation. The group writes a report and discusses what can be found in nature in the featured color. Each group gives an oral presentation of its findings, using some kind of visual aids, such as photographs, realia, or even a graphic presentation.

Based on the board book series from National Geographic, have each student select a color and draw a scene from nature to introduce the color.

Bobbie Kalman includes several activites about the senses and colors in *The Colors of Nature.* Have students analyze each sense with color. For smell, they should find objects with pleasant and unpleasant smells. Ask them what colors could be associated with the smell. Then have them write a poem about the color and the smell. For sound, they should pick a color and try to find a song that matches it. Ask them why they chose that particular song. For taste, they match colors with particular tastes, such as bitter, sweet, sour, spicy, tangy, or hot.

After discussing how nature is filled with many unique shapes as shown in Feldman's *Shapes in Nature* and Brown's *Listen to a Shape,* divide the class into small groups of two or three. Each group finds shapes in nature and documents them by taking photographs or videos or through some other visual means. Compile the group projects in a class book about nature and shapes.

Make a set of large-sized shapes, as shown on the first page of *Shapes, Shapes, Shapes* by Tana Hoban. Hold up each shape and ask the students to name the shapes before sharing the book. Explain that as you show the photographs in the book, they must try to locate the various shapes in the pictures.

After sharing the Hoban books, have a shape scavenger hunt. Make a stack of 3 × 5 cards, each with different shapes. Divide the class into teams and distribute the cards, so that each team must find objects in the classroom (or any designated area) that match the shapes on the cards.

After sharing *Round & Round & Round* by Tana Hoban, try to find even more round objects. Have the class brainstorm and create a list of all kinds of round things.

Give each student the activity sheet "Round As." Compile the students' activity sheets to create a "Round As" book.

Have the children brainstorm a list of colorful fruits and vegetables. Divide the class into small groups and assign each group four to eight of the items on the list. Have each group find or draw pictures of the items on their list. Compile the groups' work into a class "Growing Colors" book.

Plan a class visit to a greenhouse, conservatory, or plant store, where students will learn about colorful plants.

Use face paint to paint flower faces on the children or have them draw flower faces on paper.

Read *Planting a Rainbow* by Lois Ehlert to the class. Use pictures from catalogs, magazines, seed packages, and so on to help students create a set of flower cards. Have them glue the pictures on cardboard, tagboard, or old file folders, then have them sort the flowers by color. Review with them the concepts of primary or secondary colors. Instead of making flower card sets, you may wish to use the flower cutouts to make a class mural, "Rainbow of Plants."

Have students plan their own colorful flower and/or vegetable garden. Distribute the activity sheet, "Garden Map," to help them map out a garden and where different colors might be found. This activity can be adapted for older students, who could plan a multiple-season flower garden in which flowers bloom spring, summer, and fall.

With students' help, make a class chart of the different ways that flowers and vegetables are planted (e.g., bulbs in fall or seeds in spring). Ask students to list the types of flowers under the different categories. Talk about the different ways that plants grow, such as underground, as bushes, as vines, or as trees.

Try the experiment on page 28 in *Roses Red, Violets Blue: Why Flowers Have Colors.* This experiment shows how the color of anthocyanin pigments can change.

In *Sea Shapes,* various shapes transform themselves into all kinds of sea creatures. Using either the sea theme or some other theme (such as farm or jungle), choose a shape to transform into a familiar animal or object. Follow the pattern set up in the book by Suse McDonald. Use the transformed figures as part of a collage or mural about the sea.

Find pictures of all kinds of things associated with the sea and create a bulletin board of sea colors (or forest, jungle, farm, etc.).

Discuss some of the color comparisons Heidi Groennel presents in *Colors*. Have the children brainstorm to create their own list of comparisons.

After sharing *The Greedy Triangle* by Marilyn Burns, talk about triangles and other polygons. Discuss common geometric names (triangle, square, rectangle) and uncommon ones (quadrilateral, pentagon, hexagon). Discuss what happens to the triangle as it adds angles and lines.

Based on the ideas in *The Greedy Triangle,* have students create polygon pictures. Cut out various kinds of polygons. Have students choose one of the polygons and glue the shape on a sheet of paper. They must visualize the polygon as a part of a whole object, integrating the polygon into their picture of a familiar object or scene.

Share *Ten Black Dots* by Donald Crews. Have groups write a companion book using a different shape and/or color. Some examples might include "Ten Black Squares," or "Ten Green Triangles." Students in each group brainstorm a list of things found in the selected shape. They use these ideas to create a concept book.

Share some books that show geometric shapes found all around us, such as *Shapes, Shapes, Shapes* by Hoban, *Shapes* by Kightley, or *Look Around!* by Fisher. Give each student the activity sheet, "Everyday Shapes," and encourage them to look for the different shapes that can be found in everyday surroundings.

Using the basic garden shape below, plant a garden that would be filled with colors throughout the year.

MY GARDEN

Round As

Think of something that is round and compare it with another round thing. Draw a picture in the circle below and write a sentence or two about your picture.

Shapes are all around us. Look around the room, your house, the playground, etc. Find things that are in different shapes and fill in the chart with words or drawings of items that you found.

SHAPE	WHAT I FOUND
CIRCLE:	
SQUARE:	
RECTANGLE:	
TRIANGLE:	
OVAL:	
DIAMOND	
STAR:	
CRESCENT:	
HEART:	
ARC:	
ZIGZAG:	
SEMICIRCLE:	

7

GAMES, MYSTERIES, AND PUZZLES IN COLOR AND SHAPE BOOKS

Many color and shape concept books go beyond the simple identification of objects and tantalize the reader with the hint of a mystery or game. They challenge the reader to become an active participant by finding the hidden objects, guessing the correct answer, or putting the pieces of a puzzle back together. These interactive books force the reader to look beyond the literal meaning of the words and to think and see relationships among words, concepts, and daily life.

Finding the hidden object is a very popular type of puzzle used in books. In illustrator Daniel Hochstatter's *Sammy Finds the Colors* and *Sammy Searches for Shapes and Sizes,* the reader must help the shepherd and Sammy, the sheep, find objects on each page. Both of these books are very similar to the "I Spy" picture riddle books and the ever-popular "Where's Waldo" books. On the left side of each double-page spread, the concept is shown in very large letters along with a list of objects that the reader must find on the facing page. In addition to finding the name of the object, the child must find a small, colorful drawing of the object within a scene of a busy place with dozens of small objects and people. The reader must also find Sammy and the shepherd in the scene. For example, in *Sammy Finds the Colors,* for the color red, the reader must find a lobster, ball, apple, sneaker, hot dog, fire hydrant, and a rose in a neighborhood scene in which a fire engine races through the streets. When Sammy looks for rectangles in a busy neighborhood, he must find a telephone booth, bar of soap, shopping bag, fish tank, pizza, and a grape box. In addition to finding all the hidden objects, the reader can find other objects in the featured color or shape and discuss how they fit into the picture. While both books might be a bit intimidating for preschoolers, they can provide hours of fun for older readers, including adults.

For preschoolers, *Is It Red?* would be a more suitable hidden object book. A board book, it has sturdy cardboard pages and color tabs across the top of each page. The text on the left introduces a color by showing several objects in the color. The reader must then find the objects on the right-hand page along with an object in the previous color. The hidden objects are very easy to find and reinforce each color concept.

Everyone loves guessing games, and several titles use guessing as a way to reinforce color and shapes concepts. For the very young, Thomas Zacharias offers a simple game of hide-and-seek in *But Where Is the Green Parrot?* The text describes the scene on the page and always asks the reader to find the green parrot. While the bright cheerful pages are filled with such colorful objects as a pink tablecloth, yellow plate, or blue mug, it is up to the reader to find the green parrot in the pictures. The Children's Televison Workshop's *Big Bird's Color Game* is another guessing game book useful with preschoolers. This sturdy board book features Big Bird from the popular television series, *Sesame Street.* Big Bird wants the reader to guess which object on the facing page he is thinking about. He gives simple clues, but the reader may simply guess, turn the page, and the answer is revealed along with a clue about another colorful object.

Shapes are the topic of the guessing games in *Guess What?* by Beau Gardner and *Mouse Views: What the Class Pet Saw* by Bruce McMillan. In *Guess What?* the reader must try to guess the identity of an animal. On one page a box shows a shape that is part of an unknown animal. It is only after turning the page that the entire animal is revealed. In *Mouse Views,* the class mouse escapes from his house and runs rampart around the school. Through his travels, the mouse encounters a variety of lines, shapes, and textures as he wanders around the building. The photographic puzzles follow the escaped mouse through the school while depicting such common school items as scissors, paper, books, and chalk. The reader is challenged to identify the familiar objects in the colorful photographs as seen from the viewpoint of a mouse. A map in the back shows the path of the wandering mouse before he is captured and returned to his home. McMillan's illustrations always offer a unique look at the real world, but in *Mouse Views,* he has outdone himself by looking at the world from the perspective of a mouse.

What Am I? by N. N. Charles combines colors, shapes, and types of fruit in a clever guessing game. Simple, playful rhymes and die-cut shapes encourage the reader to guess the name of the fruit. As the page opens, the reader sees varying shades of the featured color on the left, while the facing page shows a die-cut shape and a rhyme that gives clues about the fruit. The reader must try to guess the name of the colorful fruit before turning the page. Vibrant, bold graphics in photographic detail show the tempting fruit on a bush, tree, or vine. Charles ends the book by referring to "a rainbow of the human race." This beautifully designed book introduces several concepts in an entertaining way.

In *The Secret Birthday Message* by Eric Carle, a little boy must unscramble the code in order to find his birthday surprise. A mysterious letter in "shape code" leads Tim on an adventure through a cave, tunnel, and other places where a birthday surprise awaits him. The cleverly designed colorful pages with shape cutouts combine a simple suspenseful story with instructions to follow, position words, shapes to match, and even simple map reading. Carle's book is more than a shape book; it is a wonderful adventure with a surprise ending.

Suse McDonald uses visual transformations as part of many of her books, and in *Sea Shapes,* she uses geometric shapes as the basis for the story. The text is very simple with only an identification of the featured shapes. Across the bottom of the left page are three boxes: the first box contains the simple shape that transforms into a sea creature, shown in its habitat on the facing page. The cut-paper collages in the underwater scene are colorful and realistic. A circle becomes the eye of a sperm whale, a spiral is part of a shark's-eye snail, and a diamond shows up as catfish scales. In the back, McDonald offers more details on each of the sea creatures and their habitats. McDonald offers an uncharacteristic look at how simple geometric shapes are a part of ordinary scenes.

Cathryn Falwell uses a similar type of visual transformation in *Clowning Around.* An ingenious clown juggles letters and shapes that transmute into other words. "Go" becomes "dog" and "dog" jumping through a circular hoop becomes "doll," etc. The crisp, bright graphics against a shiny white background makes this an eye-catching book for showing off shapes. The idea of manipulating letter pieces into new words may be too complex for young children, but the idea of shapes transforming makes *Clowning Around* an example of visual transformation that children will enjoy.

Solving a mystery is a device Running Press uses in its Fit-a-Shape series. Each small, sturdy board book in the series comes with a small plastic box filled with five plastic pieces that the reader must match with the correct image on the page. In *Colors* the reader must find the correct piece and match it to a cutout shape to answer the question, "What color is the _____?" *Shapes* also asks the reader a question that she or he answers by placing the plastic piece into the correct shape.

A series of sturdy board books from Snapshot (Covent Garden Books) combines concepts and object recognition with puzzles. Each page includes a chunky puzzle that matches the shape or color featured on the facing page. A thin color border surrounds the photographs of familiar objects on each page. In *Color Puzzles* a small object in that color is found scattered around the page and in each of the four colors. Ladybugs dot the red pages, blueberries appear on the blue page, flowers drape over the yellow page, and inchworms creep across the green page. On the left are small photographs of familiar objects, including word identifications. On the right are pop-out puzzle pieces of familiar things. On the red page, puzzle pieces of red fruit include a strawberry, raspberry, apple, and cherries, which each can be removed and placed back on the page. A similar format is used in *Shape Puzzles,* with colorful shapes used on the puzzle page and photographs of familiar objects on the facing page. For circles, readers can identify a cupcake, cookies, yo-yo, lollipop, and drum as they remove the four colorful puzzle pieces and fit them back into their proper places. Taking the puzzle pieces out of the puzzle and then popping them back in again make these two titles books that a child will return to over and over.

Matching colors and shapes is the topic of two titles by Keith Faulkner. Both books include a die-cut plastic pocket on the front of each book, which holds the color pieces and push-out shapes. Readers use the pieces to match colors and shapes throughout the books. In *My First Pick-n-Match Book of Colors,* a series of colorful boxes across the top of each page shows how the color gradually changes from one shade to another by blending. For example, yellow changes to golden yellow to light yellow, then dark orange, then red and deep red, continuing on to blend with other colors to form even more shades and combinations. Faulkner also explains the concept of primary and secondary colors and shows how they combine to form shades. Each page shows familiar objects in the various color shades along with color and word identification and a patch to match with one from the box. On the final page, the colored shapes must be placed in the proper spot to complete the jungle picture. *My First Pick-n-Match Book of Shapes* uses a similar format except that shape patches complete parts of pictures. For example, a diamond shape may complete a kite; a circle for the sun, and a triangle for a sailboat. The final page is a grid surrounded by pictures that show how different shapes can be put together to make up more objects. Both of these books are excellent tools for interactive participation and reinforcing beginning concepts. Puzzles and games appeal to readers of all ages, and they are very effective methods to use in introducing concepts about color and shapes because they generate high levels of interest.

BIBLIOGRAPHY

Colors

Big Bird's Color Game. Illustrated by Tom Cooke. New York: CTW/Golden, 1989, 1990. ISBN 0-307-12254-9.
Big Bird invites the reader to try and guess what object he is thinking about as he introduces colors.

Color Puzzles. New York: Covent Garden Books, 1996. ISBN 0-7894-0615-2.
This book combines commonplace objects and color puzzles in one easy book.

Colors. Philadelphia: Running Press, 1996. ISBN 1-56138-707-X.
Readers match the plastic play pieces with the correct colors.

Faulkner, Keith. *My First Pick-n-Match Book of Colors*. Illustrated by Jonathan Lambert. New York: Barnes and Noble Books, 1994. ISBN 1-56619-498-9.
By mixing and matching colored patches, a child learns all about colors.

Is it Red? Stephanie Longfoot, illustrator. Newmarket, England: Brimax Books, 1993. ISBN 0-86112-973-3.
In addition to learning about colors, the reader must find colorful hidden objects in each picture.

MacKinnon, Debbie. *Eye Spy Colors*. Photographs by Anthea Sieveking. Watertown, Massachusetts: Charlesbridge Publishing, 1998. ISBN 0-88106-334-7.
Look through the peephole and try to guess the answer in this surprising book about colors.

Sammy Finds the Colors. Daniel J. Hochstatter, illustrator. Nashville, Tennessee: Thomas Nelson Publishers, 1994. ISBN 0-7852-7994-6.
Learn your colors and find Sammy, the sheep, in this distinctive hidden-objects book.

Sis, Peter. *Going Up: A Color Counting Book*. New York: Greenwillow Books, 1989. ISBN 0-688-08125-8; 0-688-08127-6 (pbk).
As Mary rides up the elevator, she is joined by a colorful array of people bound for a surprise birthday party.

What Color Will Bear Wear? Mahwah, New Jersey: Troll Associates, 1989. ISBN 0-8167-1602-1.
As Bear gets dressed, the reader guesses which color of clothing he will choose next.

Zacharias, Thomas. *But Where Is the Green Parrot?* Illustrated by Wanda Zacharias. New York: Delacorte Press, 1965, 1990. ISBN 0-385-30091-3; 0-385-30111-1 (lib bdg).
On the train, the ship, or in the toy chest, where is the green parrot hiding?

Shapes

Allington, Richard L. *Shapes*. Illustrated by Lois Ehlert. Milwaukee, Wisconsin: Raintree Publishers, Inc., 1979. ISBN 0-8172-1277-9 (lib bdg).
This informative book introduces twenty different geometric shapes.

Blackstone, Stella. *Bear in a Square*. Illustrated by Debbie Harter. New York: Barefoot Press, 1998. ISBN 1-901223-58-2.
In this introduction to squares and counting, a bear roams the pages in search of adventure.

Carle, Eric. *The Secret Birthday Message*. New York: HarperCollins Publishers, 1971. ISBN 0-690-72347-4; 0-690-72348-2 (lib bdg).
Tim finds a secret message in code that sends him on a treasure hunt for his birthday surprise.

Falwell, Cathryn. *Clowning Around*. New York: Orchard Books, 1991. 0-531-05952-9; 0-531-08552-X (lib bdg).
An ingenious clown turns letters and shapes into words and pictures.

Faulkner, Keith. *My First Pick-n-Match Book of Shapes*. Illustrated by Jonathan Lambert. New York: Barnes and Noble Books, 1994. ISBN 1-56619-498-9.
Match the colorful push-out shapes and learn to recognize and name shapes.

Gardner, Beau. *Guess What?* New York: Lothrop, Lee and Shepard Books, 1985. ISBN 0-688-04982-6; 0-688-04983-4 (lib bdg).
Children guess the name of the animal from its colorful shape.

McDonald, Suse. *Sea Shapes*. Orlando, Florida: Harcourt, Brace & Co., 1994. ISBN 0-15-200027-5.
In this undersea world, shapes transform themselves into all kinds of sea creatures.

McMillan, Bruce. *Mouse Views: What the Class Pet Saw*. New York: Holiday House, 1993. ISBN 0-8234-1008-0.
When the class mouse escapes from his house, he encounters lines, shapes, and textures of all sorts as he wanders through the rooms.

Rogers, Paul. *The Shapes Games*. Pictures by Sian Tucker. New York: Henry Holt and Co., Inc., 1989. ISBN 0-8050-1280-X.

A bouncy, rhyming riddle introduces shapes around us.

Sammy Searches for Shapes and Sizes. Daniel J. Hochstatter, illustrator. Nashville, Tennessee: Thomas Nelson Publishers, 1994. ISBN 0-0-7852-7993-8.

The reader helps Sammy find objects hidden in each colorful picture.

Shape Puzzles. New York: Covent Garden Books, 1996. ISBN 0-7894-0614-4.

Find a big red circle or find a small blue star in this jigsaw puzzle book.

Shapes. Philadelphia: Running Press, 1996. ISBN 1-56138-709-6.

The child matches the shape to the picture on each page.

Colors and Shapes

Blackstone, Stella, *Can You See the Red Balloon?* Illustrated by Debbie Harter. New York: Orchard Books, 1997. ISBN 0-531-3077-3.

The reader has to find all sorts of colorful objects and Florence the cow in this playful book.

Charles, N. N. *What Am I? Looking through Shapes at Apples and Grapes.* Illustrated by Leo and Diane Dillon. New York: The Blue Sky Press, 1994. ISBN 0-590-47891-5.

Playful riddles and die-cut shapes interest students in this guessing game about colors and fruits.

Wells, Tony. *Allsorts: A Preschool Puzzle Book.* New York: Aladdin Books, 1987. ISBN 0-689-71185-9.

This hidden-object puzzle book for preschoolers includes the search for colors and shapes.

After sharing *The Secret Birthday Message* by Eric Carle, have each student create their own rebus birthday card using a variety of shapes as part of the message.

In *The Secret Birthday Message,* the shape clues helped Tim find his new pet. Give each child several different shapes (e.g., circle, triangles, squares) and use the shapes to draw a pet on the activity sheet, "Shape Pets." Be sure to write the name of the shape on the back of the shape when using this activity with very young children.

Just as Suse McDonald uses visual transformations in *Sea Shapes,* have each student use a familiar shape and transform it into a familiar animal. The activity sheet, "Transformations," will serve as a guide.

Riddles and die-cut shapes reveal colorful fruits in *What Am I?* by N. N. Charles. Choose another category and have students write a riddle about an object, giving clues based on its color and purpose. You might start by using foods, such as vegetables or sweets. Use large cutouts of shapes to inspire students to write guessing shape riddles.

Before reading *Mouse Views* by Bruce McMillan, explain that the story is from the mouse's point of view. As you show the pictures, have the children try to identify the objects in the photographs. Write another adventure for the escaped mouse.

Share *Mouse Views* with middle school students. Divide the class into small groups of two or three. Ask each group to choose a familiar place and photograph parts of the area, showing shapes, lines, and textures from a mouse's perspective. The close-up photographs should only reveal a small portion of the object. Have the other students in the class try to identify the objects in the photographs.

Paul Rogers' *The Shapes Games* used the old "I Spy" game to identify shapes. Play the game using shapes in your classroom or playground and have students guess the shapes.

Have students make their own color or shape puzzle scene, similar to those in the pick-n-match books by Keith Faulkner. Supply students with various color and shape patches to complete their pictures.

Hold a color or shape scavenger hunt. Divide the class into teams of two or three. Give each team a list of color or shape objects to find. The lists can be identical or different. When the teams find all the items on their list, classify the items by color, function, size, or shape. Make charts of each classification and discuss the hunt and its results.

Distribute to each child a scramble puzzle, such as "Colorful Word Scramble" or "Shape Scramble," to solve.

Shape Pets

Using one or more of the following shapes, create your own shape pet. (Circle, triangle, square, diamond, and rectangle).

Draw a simple shape. Change it in two stages to make a familiar animal or object. Then draw a picture that shows the animal or object in its natural setting.
For example:

Colorful Word Scramble

Find and circle the name of each color in the puzzle below. The words can be found up and down, across or diagonal, and spelled either forward or backward.

BEIGE	INDIGO	RED
BLACK	LAVENDER	ROSE
BLUE	MAGENTA	SCARLET
BROWN	ORANGE	SILVER
FUCHSIA	PEACH	TAN
GOLD	PINK	TURQUOISE
GRAY	PURPLE	VIOLET
GREEN	RAINBOW	WHITE
YELLOW		

```
Y T U I O R A N G E H
E E D B T E L R A C S
G O L D A B I N A G B
I U J L N R K E C R S
E T E F O O P N Y E L
B L A C K W H I T E A
R E D F G N P J S N V
A I T U R Q U O I S E
I N X C A H R B L P N
N D J H Y Z P K V I D
B I E S O R L M E N E
O G V I O L E T R K R
W O P A M A G E N T A
```

Find and circle the name of each shape in the puzzle below. The words can be found up and down, across or diagonal, and spelled either forward or backward.

CIRCLE	HEART	SEMICIRCLE
CONE	HEXAGON	SPHERE
CRESCENT	OCTAGON	SQUARE
CROSS	OVAL	STAR
CUBE	PENTAGON	TRIANGLE
CYLINDER	PYRAMID	ZIGZAG
DIAMOND	RECTANGLE	

```
P E N T A G O N K O
H Y M H A C C O N E
O T R E N U Y N K R
V S T A R B L O Y A
A C F R M E I G E U
L B O T V I N A L Q
D N O M A I D X G S
Z I G Z A G E E N C
C I R C L E R H A R
O C T A G O N C T O
C R E S C E N T C S
N T R I A N G L E S
X E T M S P H E R E
S E M I C I R C L E
```

8

EXPLORING COLORS AND SHAPES IN STORIES

Stories are a quintessential element in a child's young life, and they offer many opportunities to introduce literary concepts such as character and plot, to develop an awareness of the power of the written word, and to reinforce basic concepts. One way to explore the world of colors and shapes is through stories, whether it is in a formal setting like a classroom or library or in an informal way such as a bedtime story. A story may focus on one color such as *The Pink Party* by Maryann McDonald and *Harold and the Purple Crayon* by Crockett Johnson using the single color (or two) throughout the book as an integral part of the plot. In other cases an entire rainbow of colors may be the subject of the plot such as *Purple, Green and Yellow* by Robert Munsch. The identification of colors or shapes might be the focal point of the plot, or one integral element of the story.

In many cases, a story may concentrate on one color that ties together the action. In *The Pink Party,* by Maryann McDonald, best friends Amy and Lisa both love the color pink. They collect all sorts of pink things, until jealousy rears its head over who has the most. The girls manage to resolve their feelings and still remain friends. The illustrations are filled with soft, warm colors and many shades of pink to emphasize how important the color is to the plot. McDonald has written a story about friendship with the color pink as the key for the plot device. Purple is the color emphasized in *Harold and the Purple Crayon,* by Crockett Johnson, and *The Purple Coat,* by Amy Hest. Harold takes his trusty purple crayon everywhere and uses it to save himself from many mishaps. In *The Purple Coat,* Gabby is determined to get a purple coat instead of the navy one that her mother insists upon every year. Hest interweaves many other colors, such as red painted fingernails and golden pumpkins, through-

out the story, but purple is the focus of the tale. Gabby gets opinions from everyone in her family about the new coat, and finally convinces her mother that purple is the perfect color.

Valrie Selkowe has written a cheerful tale about a duck with a problem in *Spring Green.* Danny searches high and low for something special to take to a "green" contest at a spring party. His friend, Ricket the frog, has the same problem. So the two put their heads together and decide to go to the party using the frog as Danny's special "green" thing. All of the illustrations are filled with shades of green, presenting the reader with an opportunity to think about the different hues and tones of a color. Red and green are the focus of a new edition of Margaret Wise Brown's classic tale about traffic lights, *Red Light, Green Light.* First published in 1945, this timeless tale was reissued with updated illustrations. The traffic light blinks its stop-and-go message all day long. The red and green lights flash as the road is filled with action on alternate pages of text of *Red Light, Green Light. The Red Ball* by Joanna Yardley blends the past and the present using a red ball to tie the generations together. Joanie follows her dog Max and finds herself drawn into an imaginative visit to the past. The photographs start with a picture of a baby and a red ball. The baby grows and changes until the final photograph shows Joanie's grandmother, mother, and a baby along with the red ball. The three-dimensional pictures with the red ball make Yardley's story a good read-aloud about families.

At one time or another, everyone chooses a favorite color and shape. It may be because of the way the color or shape looks or how it makes someone feel or even because a favorite animal, piece of clothing, or object is in that color. In *Red Is Best,* by Kathy Stinson, a little girl describes all the reasons why red is the best color. Her mother counters every statement with one about a different color, but she never convinces her daughter that red is not the best. Mary Serfozo also extols the virtues of the color red in *Who Said Red?* A little girl teases her younger brother as he searches for his red kite. She tries to convince her brother that other colors are just as good as red. But no matter how many examples she gives about a color, her brother sticks to his favorite. In Roger Duvoisin's story, *See What I Am,* the colors argue over which one is the best. Max, the cat, serves as the narrator as each color makes a list of all the objects found in the color. The attributes of each color are listed on the left side of each page, while the right side shows how the world would look in that color. In the end, the colors agree that together they make the world beautiful, and the last page shows the same picture with a rainbow of colors. Duvoisin has written a story about getting along and working together, and at the same time he introduces the concept of color. Getting along is the theme of *Squares Are Not Bad!* by Violet Salazar. Squares, circles, and rectangles get into an argument about who is best. One day the circle falls down a hill onto a rectangle and forms a wagon. Through that accident along with other mishaps, the shapes discover that by combining they can create plenty of pretty things.

Feelings play a part in the selection of a favorite color. Patricia Hubbard uses a box of crayons to discuss colors and feelings in *My Crayons Talk*. In this happy bouncy tale, a little girl tells how her crayons talk, shout, swing, and hoot about feelings. The illustrator used crayons, gouache, acrylics, and pencil to create the exuberant pictures. From a brown mud-pie day to red roars, colors, feelings, pictures, and words bounce, jostle, and leap across the pages in this celebration of color. Colors and emotions are the central theme of *My Many Colored Days* by Dr. Seuss. This simple rhyming story was written in 1973, but not published until 1996. It was illustrated (at Dr. Seuss's request) by an artist who could bring the story to life with illustrations that were very different from his. Dr. Seuss (Theodor Geisel) found the constantly changing patterns of light and color fascinating and liked to compare the color of the day to his own emotional state. The typical, simple, and expressive rhyme of Dr. Seuss is accompanied by vivid, expressive paintings that depict the mood for each color. A

menagerie of animals and a wide spectrum of colors are used throughout the book to help the bouncy rhyme show exactly the emotion each color evokes. *My Many Colored Days* is a excellent title describing colors and emotions.

A little boy describes how a color day feels in *I Feel Orange Today* by Patricia Godwin. In addition to orange, he describes green as a quiet day and red as a tiring one. The cartoonish watercolor illustrations offer a cheerful look at how colors make us feel. Although the ending is a bit simplistic, Godwin describes most days as a rainbow, a combination of all kinds of feelings. A happy frog experiments with colors and feelings in *Rainbows and Frogs* by Joy Kim. All sorts of familiar objects in the colors red, yellow, green, orange, and blue are explored in this discussion of how colors make us feel. Perhaps the best book to explore colors and feelings is *The Gift of Driscoll Lipscomb* by Sara Yamaka. Each year, Driscoll Lipscomb the painter gives Molly a pot of color from the rainbow and a paintbrush as her wand. Molly spends the year painting with the one color that Driscoll has given her. She describes how the color makes her feel as she learns to capture the wonders of the world and see life from different angles. In the end, Molly receives the biggest gift of all when she discovers Driscoll's most cherished secret, which changes her life forever.

Several picture books for older readers focus on colors and shapes as an essential part of the story, but only as a means of conveying a more far-reaching message. For example, *The Boy Who Spoke Colors,* by David Gifaldi, is about the nature of power and talent rather than a tale of colors. When Felix tries to speak, rich vibrant colors emerge instead of words. The greedy king decides to kidnap Felix so he can bottle the colors Felix speaks, sell them, and make himself rich. In the end, the plot backfires, and the king's greed seals his doom. While colors are certainly the focal point of the story, the theme of this original folktale is exploitation and greed. The lavish, vibrant illustrations go hand in hand with the greed of the king and his desire to exploit Felix.

Harlequin and the Gift of Many Colors is a picture book version of the Harlequin tale, introducing colors and shapes. The diamond-shaped pattern of Harlequin's costume is well known, but early drawings show that it was originally a suit with irregular patterns sewn together. Harlequin's friends get together and decide to give him a new patchwork suit for Carnival. Each friend gives a small piece of cloth that ends up in his new colorful costume. Although *Harlequin and the Gift of Colors,* by Remy Charlip and Burton Supree, is not a color and shape identification book, both concepts play a part in the story. The colorful pieces of cloth are sewn together in a diamond pattern, offering the reader the opportunity to discuss the arrangement of colors and the diamond pattern in the cloak. The relationship between geometric shapes is important in *A Cloak for the Dreamer,* by Aileen Friedman. A tailor asks each of his three sons to create a cloak for the archduke. Two of the sons create beautiful cloaks using squares and rectangles, sewn snugly together, while the third son, Misha, makes a cloak of circles and open spaces, showing his desire for travel instead of a life as a tailor. *A Cloak for the Dreamer* uses shapes as one means of conveying a larger message about individuality and choosing lifestyles.

Color and shapes play an important role in several other folktale stories. Diz Wallis has created an introduction to the emotive world of color in *Mandarins and Marigolds: A Child's Journey through Color.* In this beautiful poetry story, a young boy explores the world of colors in his home and the world around him. The watercolor landscapes are filled with vibrant rich colors and many objects that are tied into the featured color. Each page emphasizes a particular brilliant hue that builds to the final image of a rainbow leaping across the earth. *The Rainbow Princess and the Land of Black and White,* by T. G. Ponte, uses a folktale style to tell the story of lost seeds. The rainbow trees are grown on Rainbow Island, and everyday their seeds are harvested and sent all over the earth to become beautiful rainbows. One day Princess Iana and her friends, the Acharuco Indians, awake to find that someone has stolen the seeds and turned the colorful island into a land of black and white. They must venture into the unknown to recover the seeds or the world's color is lost forever. Colors are the focal point of the story, but *The Rainbow Princess and the Land of Black and White* is not a color identification book. In a take-off of an old classic, Grace Maccarone concentrates on shapes to tell *The Silly Story of Goldie Locks and the Three Squares.* In this tale, a descendant of the famous Goldilocks goes for a walk in the woods and comes upon a stranger's house. Just like her ancestor, she can't resist temptation and goes

inside for a look. She doesn't like the noodles in two of the bowls, but she finds the square bowls just to her liking. She has trouble with the different-shaped chairs and beds until she finds a shape that is just right. The story follows the basic pattern of the traditional tale, but with a geometric twist. This book is a part of a Hello Math series, and it includes many activities in the back to help children think more about shapes and geometric ideas.

Because paint, colors, and houses seem to go hand in hand, it is only natural that these two topics are the focus of several books. One of the best is *Oh, Were They Ever Happy!* by Peter Spier. Three children are left all alone one afternoon when the babysitter fails to show up. They decide to surprise their parents by painting the outside of the house. From that point on, things proceed very smoothly (at least from the children's point of view). With plenty of paint (different colors in each can), ladders, and brushes, the children have everything that they need. They even clean up and put the empty cans out for the trash man. Of course, the problem is will their parents like the rainbow-colored house? Spier has a wonderful way of telling a story through his colorful illustrations accompanied by only minimal text. *Oh, Were They Ever Happy!* is a delightful tale to read aloud and talk about colors.

Creating an unusual look for a house is the subject of *The Big Orange Splot* by Daniel Manus Pinkwater. When a seagull drops orange paint on his house, Mr. Plumbean decides to create an entirely new look for his home. Instead of repainting it to look like the rest of the houses on his block, Mr. Plumbean paints it to reflect his dreams. He turns his simple house into a rainbow of jungle colors. At first, his neighbors are upset, but one by one they decide to change the look of their houses and make each one reflect the dreams of its owners. Leonard Kessler uses a similar story line in *Mr. Pine's Purple House.* Mr. Pine decides to make his house stand out in the row of white houses on Vine Street, so he paints it purple. After Mr. Pine decides to make a statement with a purple house, his neighbors also decided to paint their houses to reflect their personalities. Using only black and white line drawings with accents of purple, Kessler has written a simple, satisfying story about being an individual.

Changing the look of a house is the theme of *Pig's Orange House,* by Ethel and Leonard

Kessler, and *The House of Four Seasons,* by Roger Duvoisin. When Pig decides to paint her house orange, her well-meaning friends go a little too far. As they try to mix orange, somehow they end up with purple and green too. A little miscommunication results in a multicolored house. The simple comic illustrations and humorous plot make *Pig's Orange House* a good story to introduce mixing colors to create even more colors. In *The House of Four Seasons,* Roger Duvoisin tells the story of a family trying to decide what color to paint the old house they bought. Each member of the family imagines the house in a different color to go with one of the four seasons. With a little finesse and a simple color trick, Father finally gets everyone to agree that white is a color for all seasons. Duvoisin's story was published over forty years ago, but it is as fresh as the day it was published.

In *The House That Makes Shapes,* by Jim Potts, the topic turns from colors to shapes. When a little boy goes for a walk, he comes upon a house that makes shapes. As the boy presses a button, he creates all sorts of shapes. However, the more shapes that he makes, the bigger the mess becomes. It takes some doing, but finally the boy decides what to do with all the extra shapes. The modernistic illustrations introduce five basic shapes to the reader with ideas on how different shapes make up larger shapes.

Discovering colors on a walk is a popular topic for stories. In the classic tale, *Harold and the Purple Crayon* (Crockett Johnson), Harold takes his trusty purple crayon on a moonlight walk. The purple crayon comes in handy to make pies when he is hungry, to save him from a number of mishaps and finally to help Harold get home. Crockett Johnson focuses on only one color throughout this "oldie but goodie" tale of a little boy and his imagination. In *Tom's Rainbow Walk,* by Catherine Anholt, Tom tries to decide what color his new sweater should be. As his Grandma knits, Tom takes a nap and dreams about colors through a walk in the garden. In his dream he questions all the animals about their favorite colors, while trying to make a decision of his own. In the end, Tom decides that he likes all the colors, and surprise! Grandma has made a rainbow sweater.

In *A Winter Walk,* by Lynne Barasch, Sophie and her mother go on a walk one cold gray winter day and discover that winter is filled with colors. Sophie's mother shows her how to look beyond the grayness and discover more colors of winter, such as the red berries, brown rabbits, and white falling snow. The delicate watercolor illustrations accentuate this soothing tale of the rewards of looking beyond the obvious. Sophie discovers the beauty of nature and the colors of the winter season. *Beside the Bay,* by Sheila White Samson, is the story of a little girl who takes a walk by the bay. As she walks, she is joined by a series of colorful creatures and familiar objects until the end of the walk when the bay returns to its original colors of blue and gray. Rhyming couplets and simple collage art are used in this circular tale of the bay. Nature also is the topic of *The Paint-Box Sea,* by Doris Herold Lund. Jane and her brother explore the seashore, trying to decide what is the real color of the ocean. What they discover is that the ocean is constantly changing like the colors in Jane's paint box. The rich paintings show the changing moods of the ocean from the red gold of a million goldfish to the green of a cat's eyes.

Not only are witches, ghosts, and other scary creatures popular with children of all ages, but they are also useful for introducing concepts like colors. *Winnie the Witch* by Korky Paul and Valerie Thomas is not a concept book in the true sense of the word, but it does use colors as an integral part of the plot. Winnie lives in a black house with a black cat, surrounded by black things. The problem is that every time her cat falls asleep, the cat blends in with the black background, and Winnie keeps falling over him. An exasperated Winnie turns the cat green, tosses it outside, and then falls over the cat without seeing it against the green grass. Winnie transforms her cat in a rainbow of colors, but each time it backfires. Finally, Winnie comes up a with unique and colorful solution to her problem, and of course, everyone lives happily ever after. Colors are clearly identified and used throughout the story, but they are not the central focus.

The Color Wizard by Barbara Brenner is another tale about using magic to change a single-color world into a rainbow. The wizard lives in a dull gray world. One day he discovers colors and proceeds to paint his planet from castle door to sky in every color of the rainbow. Brenner uses rhyming text and colorful illustrations by Leo and Diane Dillon to introduce colors. Notes about colors are included in the back of the book. The wizard goes wild with one color at a time in *The Great Blueness and Other Predicaments* by

Arnold Lobel. In this amusing tale, the wizard uses his paint pots to transform his dull world into a profusion of colors. First, he paints things blue, and then everyone paints everything blue. When he tires of the blueness, the wizard uses his red paint pot to paint over the blueness. Soon everyone paints everything red, then yellow. Finally, the wizard discovers that he can mix the colors in paint pots to produce even more colors and create a rainbow world that everyone enjoys.

Magic in the form of goblins and ghosts shows off colors in *Goblins in Green,* by Nicholas Heller, and *The Ghosts' Dinner,* by Jacques Duquennoy. When two children decide to explore the attic, they discover a host of ghastly green goblins getting dressed. From A to Z the twenty-six goblins gallivant across the pages wearing all sorts of interesting and colorful clothes. Cranberry dungarees, a red sarong, an indigo jersey, and violet woolies are only a few of the colors and clothes that the goblins try on. Although goblins are usually perceived as wicked, these three-dimensional goblins are human-like and cute instead of scary. In addition to familiar colors like red and blue, the goblins wear clothes in various shades of the primary colors. Heller offers a unique opportunity to identify colors and shades and to discuss the alphabet and different types of clothing. Six hungry ghosts change colors as they eat in Duquennoy's humorous tale, *The Ghosts' Dinner.* Henry invites six very hungry ghost friends over for a nice meal. But the problems begin when the ghosts change to the color of whatever food they are eating. If they drink a little spinach juice, they turn green; if they eat pumpkin soup, they turn orange; and then the main course of salmon turns the party into a parade of pink ghosts. It takes some doing, but Henry finally manages to solve the dilemma when he serves a very special dessert. Although Duquennoy never mentions colors directly, it is quite obvious that the changing colors of the ghosts are the focal point of the story.

Three colorful creatures set out to paint a wall in *Crazy Creatures Colors* by Hannah Reidy. They try very hard to paint quietly, but a free-for-all erupts when the paint begins to drip. The three primary colors soon drip together forming more colors until the creatures can't stand it, and they go crazy. Playful, rhythmic text and whimsical, colorful creatures are used throughout the book, with a foldout page at the end that shows what happens when the creatures go crazy. An entire school full of crazy colorful creatures inhabit the pages of *Monster School: Colors, Shapes and Opposites* by Andy Charman. The monsters are cute, friendly, and cuddly as they play and work with colors and shapes. For the color section, the monsters are in different colors and involved in such activities as playing with toys, staying up all night, and finding shells. In the shapes section, the colorful monsters build cubes, sail triangles, and fly kites as they bounce thorough the pages. Charman includes common colors and shapes as well as less common ones like mauve, turquoise, spirals, and zigzags. Captivating pictures, humorous rhymes, and happy hyper monsters provide a lively introduction to colors, shapes, and opposites in *Monster School: Colors, Shapes and Opposites.*

Only one monster is shown in Ed Emberley's *Go Away, Big Green Monster!* The focus of this book is to help children overcome a fear of night-time monsters, but it is also useful to introduce colors. The cleverly designed book uses die-cut pages to progressively build a monster's face, and then makes it disappear feature by feature. Bit by bit, the monster's face appears beginning with "two big yellow eyes," a "big red mouth," and a "scary green face." At that point, the child takes charge and banishes the monster, piece by piece until nothing is left. Emberley has invented an ingenious way for children to help chase away the fears of the dark.

In *A Beastly Story,* Bill Martin, Jr., and Steven Kellogg team up to tell a not-so-scary tale of a group of mice who venture into a dark dark wood. Based on a familiar phrase, "dark dark," Martin and Kellogg substitute the name of different colors for the second dark throughout the story. The four mice, Silly, Lily, Willy, and Nilly, walk through the woods and come upon a dark dark house, which turns out to be brown. They enter the door and discover a dark red staircase, a dark blue cellar, a dark purple cupboard, a dark green bottle, and finally a strange beast. They follow the strange beast into an even darker house with more dark colors, only to discover that their friends, Nick and Hank, are playing a trick. There was no strange beast, or was there? The real answer can be found on the last page. This first collaboration between two beloved creators of children's books combines the concept of colors with an exuberant tale of fun and frights.

Several color and shape stories don't fit into any set pattern, but they stand alone as examples of stories that use color or shapes as an integral part of the story and not as just an introduction to concepts. A host of shape characters invite the reader to search and find examples of them on the pages of *There's a Square: A Book about Shapes,* by Mary Serfozo. The shape characters have stick arms and legs, and even their facial features are in the featured shape. On the left side of each double-page spread is a description of the shape and an invitation to find examples of the shape in the collage illustration on the facing page. *Shopping Spree: Identifying Shapes* by Monica Weiss is part of a series about the Frimble frog family. In this volume, the Frimble frogs go shopping and find shapes all around. They even learn to talk in "shape" language. At the Sweet Shoppe, they find colored mint circles, chocolate rectangles, and jelled fruit triangles. The Frimbles soon find themselves speaking "shape" language all the time, like "close the rectangle (door)" or "eat a cinnamon circle (doughnut)."

Charles Shaw offers an unusual approach to identifying shapes in his classic tale, *It Looked Like Spilt Milk.* Dark blue backgrounds with white letter and shapes fill the pages of this imaginative look at clouds. The narrator tells some of the possibilities for the shape on the page, which turns out to be a cloud in the sky. *Dreams* by Peter Spier offers a similar look at the shapes found in clouds, but with more detail. In tall-tale style, Jack from *Meet Jack Appleknocker* by Arnold Sundgaard uses a shape to guide his life. Jack looks at the stain on his ceiling and plans his day around what shape he sees there each day. He plans something related to the shape of the stain, such as making pancakes after seeing a griddle shape or digging potatoes after seeing a sack of potatoes in the stain shape. Shapes are simply a tool to tell the story in each of these tales.

Eight sticks of chalk tell the story of a boy stranded on an island in *The Chalk Box Story,* by Don Freeman. As the story begins, the top pops off a box of chalk. One by one the colored sticks transform a blank piece of paper into a real story. Each stick contributes something to the tale with blue making the sky and ocean, yellow for the sand and sun, and even the red stick writing the words, "Help Me." Freeman's simple but soothing story offers a different look at the role colors

play in the world. A cleverly disguised lesson in colors and sizes is the topic of *The Little Red House,* by Norma J. Sawicki. A small child discovers an intriguing set of nesting houses. One by one, the colorful houses open to reveal a slightly smaller one until the final house reveals a tiny loveable bear. With each new house, a new color is revealed. Sawicki uses cumulative repetitive text in this soothing tale that is suitable for beginning readers and early exposure to color concepts. In a similar vein, Donald Crews's *Freight Train* uses different colored cars to introduce colors to the young reader. A freight train makes its way across the land with each colorful car carrying cargo from the black steam engine and orange tank car to the green cattle car and the red caboose. The text is brief, and the illustrations are filled with bright, cheerful colors.

Humor is the main ingredient in *I Want a Blue Banana!,* by Joyce and James Dunbar, and *Purple, Green and Yellow,* by Robert Munsch. In *I Want a Blue Banana!,* a family makes a visit to the supermarket. While his mother searches for her missing grocery list, a little boy makes silly demands for colorful fruits like a blue banana, red orange, and orange grapes. While Mom is distracted trying to find the lost list, the baby tosses Mom's selections out of the cart. The trial-and-error dialogue between mother and son provides an simple effective introduction to colors without the usual identification format. Robert Munsch has written a hilarious tale of a little girl and markers in *Purple, Green and Yellow.* This is not a color identification books, but a story where colors are the central theme. Brigid loves markers and colors. She promises her mother that she will not draw on herself with the "super-indelible-never-come-off-till-you're-dead-and-maybe-even-later" coloring markers, but of course the temptation is just too much. It takes a lot of work and imagination, but Brigid finally solves her problem with permanent markers. The comical, colorful illustrations and surprise ending make *Purple, Green and Yellow* a terrific color story for readers of all ages.

While simple identification books are certainly important to introduce concepts like colors and shapes, stories that integrate a concept into the plot are of equal importance. Some stories concentrate on only one color, while others use colors as the backdrop for the story.

Colors

Allen, Robert. *This Is Yellow and This Is Red*. Illustrated by Edith Witt. New York: Platt and Munk, Publishers, 1968.
A little boy discusses what he likes about each color.

Anholt, Catherine. *Tom's Rainbow Walk*. Boston, Massachusetts: Little, Brown and Company, 1989. ISBN 0-316-04261-7.
Grandma knits Tom a new sweater, but he can't decide what color it should be.

Asch, Frank. *Yellow Yellow*. Illustrated by Mark Alan Stamaty. New York: McGraw-Hill, 1971.
A boy returns a yellow hard hat to a worker and then goes home to make his own hat.

Baker, Alan. *Benjamin's Portrait*. New York: Lothrop, Lee and Shepard, 1986. ISBN 0-688-06877-4; 0-688-06878-2 (lib bdg).
Benjamin the hamster works on a self-portrait masterpiece with unexpected mishaps.

Barasch, Lynne. *A Winter Walk*. New York: Ticknor & Fields, 1993. ISBN 0-395-65937-1.
Sophie and her mother go on a walk and discover the colors of winter.

Bassede, Francine. *George Paints His House*. New York: Orchard Books, 1999. ISBN 0-551-30150-8.
George and Mary try to find a special color for their house.

Berenstain, Stan and Jan. *The Berenstain Bears and the Big Road Race*. New York: Random House, 1987. ISBN 0-394-89134-1; 0-394-99134-6 (lib bdg).
The bear family watches as Brother Bear's little red car competes in a road race.

Berenstain, Stan and Jan. *The Berenstain Kids: I Love Colors*. New York: Random House, 1987. ISBN 0-394-89129-5; 0-394-99129-X (lib bdg).
Two children describe in rhyme what they see in red, blue, yellow, and other colors.

Bergman, Donna. *Timmy Green's Blue Lake*. Illustrated by Ib Ohlsson. New York: Tambourine Books, 1992. ISBN 0-688-10747-8; 0-688-10748-6 (lib bdg).
When Timmy finds a blue tarp, his imagination turns it into all sorts of magical things.

Brenner, Barbara. *The Color Wizard*. Illustrated by Leo and Diane Dillon. New York: Bantam, 1989. ISBN 0-553-05825-8; 0-553-34690-3 (pbk).
Wizard Gray changes his dull, gray world into one filled with a multitude of colors.

Brown, Margaret Wise. *Red Light, Green Light*. Illustrated by Leonard Weisgard. New York: Scholastic, Inc., 1992. ISBN 0-590-44558-8.
The traffic light blinks its stop-and-go message all day long.

Crews, Donald. *Freight Train*. New York: Greenwillow Books, 1978. ISBN 0-688-80165-X; 0-688-84165-1 (lib bdg).
Brief text and illustrations follow the path of a freight train as it makes its way across the land.

DeLage, Ida. *Pink Pink*. Drawings by Benton Mahan. Champaign, Illinois: Garrard Publishing Company, 1973. ISBN 0-8116-6725-1.
A rainbow of colors winds through this cumulative tale of a little brown house and its occupants.

DePaolo, Paula. *Rosie and the Yellow Ribbon*. Illustrated by Janet Wolf. Boston, Massachusetts: Little, Brown & Co., 1992. ISBN 0-316-18100-5.
When Rosie's favorite yellow ribbon turns up missing, she thinks her best friend Lucille took it.

Dunbar, Joyce, and James Dunbar. *I Want a Blue Banana!* Boston, Massachusetts: Houghton Mifflin Company, 1991. ISBN 0-395-57579-6.
While his mother is distracted looking for her grocery list, Dan asks for all sorts of colorful fruits.

Duquennoy, Jacques. *The Ghosts' Dinner*. Racine, Wisconsin: Western Publishing Co., 1994. ISBN 0-307-17510-3.
Henry invites six hungry ghosts for a tasty, colorful dinner, but the real fun begins with a special dessert.

Duvoisin, Roger. *The House of Four Seasons*. New York: Lothrop, Lee and Shepard Co., 1956.
When a family buys an old house, they can't decide what color to paint it.

Duvoisin, Roger. *See What I Am*. New York: Lothrop, Lee and Shepard, 1974.
Each color thinks that it is the best and tells the reader why.

Emberley, Ed. *Go Away, Big Green Monster!*. Boston, Massachusetts: Little, Brown and Company, 1992. ISBN 0-316-23653-5.
Bit by bit, the big green monster appears and disappears as the reader conquers his fear of monsters.

Falwell, Cathryn. *Nicky's Walk*. New York: Clarion Books, 1991. ISBN 0-395-56914-1.
On a walk with his mother, Nicky identifies the colors of some familiar things.

Feczko, Kathy. *Umbrella Parade*. Illustrated by Deborah E. Borgo. Mahwah, New Jersey: Troll Associates, 1985. ISBN 0-8167-0356-6.
Each animal brings along a different colored umbrella for walking through the rain.

Freeman, Don. *The Chalk Box Story*. Philadelphia, Pennsylvania: J. B. Lippincott Co., 1976. ISBN 0-397-31699-2.

Eight sticks of chalk tell the story of a boy stranded on an island.

Freeman, Don. *A Rainbow of My Own*. New York: The Viking Press, 1966. ISBN 0-670-58928-4.
When a little boy tries to catch a rainbow, it remains an elusive thing.

Friskey, Margaret. *What Is the Color of the Wide, Wide World?* Chicago: Childrens Press, 1973. ISBN 0-516-03665-3.
Each animal insists that the world is a different color depending on the surroundings.

Garne, S. T. *By a Blazing Blue Sea*. Illustrated by Lori Lohstoeter. San Diego, California: Gulliver Books/ Harcourt Brace and Co., 1999. ISBN 0-15-201780-1.
Vivid illustrations and rhyming text are used to describe the colorful life of a Caribbean fisherman.

Gifaldi, David. *The Boy Who Spoke Colors*. Illustrated by C. Shana Gregor. Boston, Masschusetts: Houghton Mifflin, 1993. ISBN 0-395-65025-9.
When the king kidnaps Felix, who happens to speak in colors, the king's greed seals his doom.

Godwin, Patricia. *I Feel Orange Today*. Illustrated by Kitty Macaulay. Toronto, Ontario: Annick Press, Ltd., 1993. ISBN 1-55037-285-8.
A little boy describes how an orange day feels, as well as other color days.

Goffstein, M. B. *Artists' Helpers Enjoy the Evenings*. New York: Harper and Row Publishers, 1987. ISBN 0-06-022181-X; 0-06-022182-8 (lib bdg).
When the day is done, the artists' helpers go out and enjoy an evening together.

Graham, Bob. *The Red Woolen Blanket*. Boston, Massachusetts: Little, Brown and Company, 1987. ISBN 0-316-32310-1.
Julia carries her favorite red blanket everywhere, until one day she finally outgrows it.

Heller, Nicholas. *Goblins in Green*. Pictures by Joseph A. Smith. New York: Greenwillow Books, 1995. ISBN 0-688-12802-5 0-688-12803-3 (lib bdg).
From A to Z, a gang of colorful goblins romp in colorful garments.

Hest, Amy. *The Purple Coat*. Pictures by Amy Schwartz. New York: Four Winds Press, 1986. ISBN 0-02-743640-3.
Even though her mother insists that a navy coat is okay, Gabby wants a purple one.

Hubbard, Patricia. *My Crayons Talk*. Illustrated by G. Brian Karas. New York: Henry Holt, 1996. ISBN 0-8050-3529-X.
Colorful crayons talk, shout, swing, and hoot in this story celebrating colors and feelings.

Johnson, Crockett. *Harold and the Purple Crayon*. New York: Harper & Row Publishers, 1955. ISBN 0-06-022936-5; 0-06-443022-7 (pbk).
Harold takes his trusty purple crayon on a moonlight walk and a host of adventures.

Kessler, Ethel, and Leonard Kessler. *Pig's Orange House*. Pictures by Pat Paris. Champaign, Illinois: Garrard Publishing Co., 1981. ISBN 0-8116-7553-X.
With a little help from her friends, Pig tries to paint her house orange.

Kim, Joy. *Rainbows and Frogs: A Story about Colors*. Illustrated by Paul Harvey. Mahwah, New Jersey: Troll Associates, 1981. ISBN 0-89375-505-2 (lib bdg); 0-89375-506-0 (pbk)
A happy frog introduces colors and how they make him feel.

Kunhardt, Edith. *Red Day Green Day*. Pictures by Marilyn Hafner. New York: Greenwillow Books, 1992. ISBN 0-688-09399-X; 0-688-09400-7 (lib bdg).
Andrew and his classmates learn about colors in their kindergarten class.

Latham, Jean Lee. *What Tabbit the Rabbit Found*. Illustrated by William Dugan. Champaign, Illinois: Garrard Publishing Co., 1974. ISBN 0-8116-6052-4.
While looking for his blue ball, Tabbit finds a yellow duck, red shoe, and other missing items.

Leuck, Laura. *The Teeny Tiny Mouse*. Illustrated by Pat Schories. Mahwah, New Jersey: Bridgewater Books, 1998. ISBN 0-816-74547-1
A teeny tiny mouse finds colorful objects around the teeny tiny house.

Lobel, Arnold. *The Great Blueness and Other Predicaments*. New York: Harper & Row, Publishers, 1968. ISBN 0-06-023937-9; 0-06-023938-7 (lib bdg).
When the wizard discovers how to make colors with his paint pots, he gets carried away with one color at a time.

Lofgren, Ulf. *The Color Trumpet*. English text by Alison Winn; adapted by Ray Broekel. Reading, Massachusetts: Addison-Wesley, 1973. ISBN 0-201-04312-1.
When Ollie buys a trumpet with his birthday money, he discovers it will blow colorful bubbles.

Lund, Doris Herold. *The Paint-Box Sea*. Pictures by Symeon Shimin. New York: McGraw-Hill, 1973. ISBN 0-07-039097-5; 0-07-039098-3 (lib bdg).
Jane and her brother explore the seashore to determine the real color of the ocean.

Macdonald, Maryann. *The Pink Party*. Illustrated by Abby Carter. New York: Hyperion Books for Children, 1994. ISBN 1-56282-620-4; 1-56282-621-2 (lib bdg).
Best friends Amy and Lisa experience a little jealousy over who has the most pink things.

Mahy, Margaret. *Muppy's Ball*. Illustrated by Jan Vander Voo. Chicago: Childrens Press International, 1986. ISBN 0-516-08972-2.
Muppy enlists the aid of his colorful friends to retrieve a ball taken by an eagle.

Martin, Bill, Jr., and Steven Kellogg. *A Beastly Story*. Orlando, Florida: Silver Whistle/Harcourt Brace, 1970, 1999. ISBN 0-15-201683-X.

When four little mice venture into the dark dark wood, they find a dark brown house filled with all sorts of dark colors and a strange beast.

Martin, Janet. *Red and Blue*. Illustrated by Philippe Thomas. New York: Platt and Munk, 1965.

Curious Nick discovers all kinds of engaging facts about colors.

Moncure, Jane. *A Color Clown Comes to Town: A Book of Fun with Colors*. Illustrated by Linda Hohag and Lori Jacobson. Mankato, Minnesota: The Child's World, 1988. ISBN 0-89565-369-9.

When Laura opens a word window book, she encounters a clown with paint pots, who teachers her all about colors.

Moncure, Jane Belk. *Magic Monsters Look for Colors*. Illustrated by Diana Magnuson. Elgin, Illinois: The Child's World, 1979. ISBN 0-89565-056-8.

The magic monsters look for colors all around the town, until they find a rainbow.

Munsch, Robert. *Purple, Green and Yellow*. Illustrated by Helene Desputeaux. Toronto, Ontario: Annick Press, Ltd., 1992. ISBN 1-55037-255-6; 1-55037-256-4 (pbk).

Brigid promises not to write on herself with some special colored markers, but the temptation is too great to resist.

Muntean, Michaela. *Wet Paint: A Color Story*. Illustrated by Tom Cooke. Racine, Wisconsin: Western Publishing Co., 1990. ISBN 0-307-13115-7; 0-307-63115-X (lib bdg).

The monster painters use lots of colors to change the look of a family's house.

Paul, Korky, and Valerie Thomas. *Winnie the Witch*. Brooklyn, New York: Kane/Miller Book Publishers, 1987. ISBN 0-916291-13-8; 0-916291-32-4 (pbk).

Because Winnie lives in a house where everything is black, she can't always see her black cat, until the day she comes up with a colorful solution.

Peppe, Rodney. *The Color Catalog*. New York: Bedrick/Blackie, 1992. ISBN 0-87226-472-6.

Stripey, a black-and-white cat, goes on a spree to get some colorful clothes.

Pinkwater, Daniel Manus. *The Big Orange Splot*. New York: Hastings House Publisher, 1977. ISBN 0-8038-0777-5.

After a seagull drops orange paint on Mr. Plumbean's house, he decides to change the look of his house.

Ponte, T. G. *The Rainbow Princess and the Land of Black and White*. Illustrated by Geoffrey Brittingham. Nashville, Tennessee: Winston-Derek Publishers Group, Inc., 1996. ISBN 1-55523-730-4.

Princess Iana and her friends must find the stolen rain tree seeds or all color in the world is lost forever.

Reidy, Hannah. *Crazy Creatures Colors*. Illustrated by Clare Mackie, 1996. New York: DeAgostini Editions, Ltd., 1996. ISBN 1-899883-43-6.

Three colorful creatures try to paint the wall, but the dripping paint makes them crazy.

Samson, Sheila White. *Beside the Bay*. New York: Philomel, 1987. ISBN 0-399-21420-8.

This circular tales describes the colorful things seen on a walk beside the bay.

Sawicki, Norma Jean. *The Little Red House*. Illustrated by Toni Goffe. New York: Lothrop, Lee and Shepard Books, 1989. ISBN 0-688-07891-5; 0-688-07892-3 (lib bdg).

One at a time, the tiny toy houses reveal a new colorful house and a final surprise.

Schmidt, Bernd. *Our Friend the Painter*. Ada, Oklahoma: Garrett Educational Corporation, 1989. ISBN 0-944483-52-6.

When three children visit their painter friend, he shows them how he mixes his paints.

Selkowe, Valrie M. *Spring Green*. Pictures by Jeni Crisler Bassett. New York: Lothrop, Lee and Shepard Books, 1985. ISBN 0-688-04055-1; 0-688-04056-X (lib bdg).

Danny looks everywhere for something special to take to a "green" contest.

Serfozo, Mary. *Who Said Red?* Illustrated by Narahashi Keiko. New York: Margaret K. McElderry Books, 1988. ISBN 0-689-50455-1; 0-689-71592-7 (pbk).

A little girl tries to convince her brother that other colors are just as important as red.

Seuss, Dr. *My Many Colored Days*. Paintings by Steve Johnson and Lou Fancher. New York: Alfred A. Knopf, 1996. ISBN 0-679-87597-2; 0-679-97597-7 (lib bdg).

This simple rhyming story describes each day in terms of colors and emotions.

Sharratt, Nick. *The Green Queen*. Cambridge, Massachusetts: Candlewick Press, 1992. ISBN 1-56402-093-2; 1-56402-441-5 (pbk).

Before the queen takes her walk, she dresses in her most colorful finery.

Spier, Peter. *Oh, Were They Ever Happy!* New York: Doubleday, 1978. ISBN 0-385-13175-5; 0-385-13176-3 (prebound); 0-385-24477-0 (pbk).

When their babysitter fails to show up, the Noonan children decide to surprise their parents by painting the house.

Steig, William. *Yellow and Pink*. New York: Farrar, Straus and Giroux, 1984. ISBN 0-374-48735-9.

When two small figures find themselves lying in the sun, they imagine all kinds of reasons for being there.

Stinson, Kathy. *Red Is Best*. Art by Robin Baird Lewis. Toronto, Ontario: Annick Press, Ltd., 1982. ISBN 0-920236-24-3; 0-920236-26-X (pbk).

A little girl describes all the reasons why red is the best color.

Tison, Annette, and Talus Taylor. *The Adventures of the Three Colors.* Cleveland, Ohio: World Publishing, 1971. ISBN 0-529-01239-1

All sorts of animals and colors combine to create even more colors.

Wallis, Diz. *Mandarins and Marigolds: A Child's Journey through Color.* Milwaukee, Minnesota: Gareth Stevens Publishing, 1995. ISBN 0-8368-1391-X.

A young boy explores the world of colors in his home and the world around him.

Wylie, Joanne, and David Wylie. *A Fishy Color Story.* Chicago: Childrens Press, 1983. ISBN 0-516-02983-5.

When a little girl catches a fish, she tries to describe what color it is.

Wylie, Joanne, and David Wylie. *The Gumdrop Monster.* Chicago: Childrens Press, 1984. ISBN 0-516-04492-3.

As a little boy follows a trail of gumdrops, he encounters an assortment of colorful monsters.

Yamaka, Sara. *The Gift of Driscoll Lipscomb.* Illustrated by Joung Un Kim. New York: Simon and Schuster, 1995. ISBN 0-02-793599-X.

Each year, Driscoll Lipscomb gives Molly a pot of color from the rainbow and a paintbrush for her wand.

Yardley, Joanna. *The Red Ball.* San Diego, California: Harcourt Brace Jovanovich, 1991. ISBN 0-15-200894-2.

When Joanie follows her dog Max, she finds herself drawn into a imaginative trip to the past.

Shapes

Eberts, Marjorie, and Margaret Gisler. *Pancakes, Crackers, and Pizza.* Illustrated by Stephen Hayes. Chicago: Childrens Press, 1984. ISBN 0-516-02063-3.

The foods that Eddy loves to eat come in a variety of shapes.

Friedman, Aileen. *A Cloak for the Dreamer.* Illustrated by Kim Howard. New York: Scholastic, Inc., 1994. ISBN 0-590-48987-9.

A tailor asks his three sons to create a cloak for the archduke.

Maccarone, Grace. *The Silly Story of Goldie Locks and the Three Squares.* Illustrated by Anne Kennedy; math activities by Marilyn Burns. New York: Scholastic, Inc., 1996. ISBN 0-590-54344-X.

A descendant of the famous Goldilocks goes for a walk and enters a stranger's house.

Martin, Janet. *Round and Square.* Illustrated by Philippe Thomas. New York: Platt and Munk, 1965.

As he explores the world around him, Nick discovers the world of "rounds" and "squares."

Potts, Jim. *The House That Makes Shapes.* Tucson, Arizona: Harbinger House, 1992. ISBN 0-943173-74-4.

A little boy discovers a house that makes shapes when he presses a button.

Salazar, Violet. *Squares Are Not Bad!* Pictures by Harlow Rockwell. New York: Golden Press, 1967. ISBN 0-307-62102-2.

All the shapes can't get along until the day they discover that they can create all sorts of things by combining with one another.

Serfozo, Mary. *There's a Square: A Book about Shapes.* Illustrated by David A. Carter. New York: Scholastic, 1996. ISBN 0-590-54426-8.

A host of shape characters invite the reader to search for shapes in the pictures.

Shaw, Charles G. *It Looked Like Spilt Milk.* New York: Harper and Brothers, 1947. ISBN 0-06-025567-8; 0-06-443159-2 (pbk); 0-694-00491-X (board)

Clouds come in all shapes and sizes, limited only by the viewer's imagination.

Spier, Peter. *Dreams.* New York: Doubleday, 1986. ISBN 0-385-19336-X.

The children see all sorts of shapes in the clouds.

Sundgaard, Arnold. *Meet Jack Appleknocker.* Illustrated by Sheila White Samton. New York: Philomel Books, 1988. ISBN 0-399-21472-0.

Jack uses the shape of a stain on the ceiling to help him plan his day.

Weiss, Monica. *Shopping Spree: Identifying Shapes.* Illustrated by Rose Mary Berlin. Mahwah, New Jersey: Troll Associates, 1992. ISBN 0-8167-2490-3 (lib bdg); 0-8167-2491-1 (pbk).

The Frimble frogs go on a shopping spree and identify all kinds of shapes.

Colors and Shapes

Charlip, Remy, and Burton Supree. *Harlequin and the Gift of Colors.* New York: Parents Magazine Press, 1973. ISBN 0-8193-0494-8; 0-8193-0495-6 (lib bdg).

Harlequin's friends make him a new patchwork costume for Carnival.

Charman, Andy. *Monster School: Colors, Shapes and Opposites.* Illustrated by Sue King. New York:

Smithmark Publishers, Inc., 1995. ISBN 0-8317-5872-4.

A cast of crazy colorful creatures make learning a ton of fun ar Monster School.

Morris, Neil. *Rummage Sale: A Fun Book of Shapes and Colors*. Minneapolis, Minnesota: Carolrhoda Books, Inc., 1990. ISBN 0-87614-676-0.

While putting things out for the school rummage sale, Katie and her dad discover all sorts of shapes and colors.

STORY ACTIVITIES

Read the children some of the stories that feature one color such as *The Pink Party* by Maryann Macdonald. Discuss colors and have students make a list of their favorite colors. Make a bar or pie chart showing the colors and number of children who list it as their favorite. Another activity might be to write a story about a favorite color or even another "pink" adventure for Amy and Lisa.

Margaret Wise Brown's classic tale, *Red Light, Green Light,* is about traffic lights. Talk about the meaning of the different colors of traffic lights and other traffic symbols. Make traffic signals using a black rectangle as the background and circles for the lights. After sharing the story, play the game, "Red Light, Green Light."

A little girl decides that *Red Is Best* in the story by Kathy Stinson. Ask the children to paint a picture showing how "RED IS BEST" or any other favorite color. With older children, write a paragraph describing how, why, and ways that red (or any other color) is best.

After reading *Squares Are Not Bad!,* by Violet Salazar, give each student an assortment of rectangles, circles, squares, and triangles. Ask the children to combine the shapes to make more things and create shape pictures.

Colors can evoke a number of feelings. Share some of the stories about colors and feelings and have the class discuss how colors can evoke different feelings. Brainstorm a list of emotions and feelings that are associated with different colors.

Choose several colors to use in a survey of colors and feelings. Cut out squares of each color. Hold up the square and ask the students how that color makes you feel (warm, hot, cold, cool, etc.) Record the way that different colors make people feel. Use the results of the survey to create a graph or chart.

Read *The Gift of Driscoll Lipscomb,* by Sara Yamaka. Discuss Molly's feelings about the different colors. Yellow made Molly feel the warmth of the summer sun, misty dusks, and clear dawns. Molly learns to look at the world in terms of the colors of the rainbow. What was the gift of Driscoll Lipscomb? How did it make Molly look at the world differently?

Ask each student to select a color and write a paragraph describing the ways that the selected color looks and feels. Choose an event or personal experience associated with a specific color. Some examples might be the warm yellow sun of a day at the beach, the cold still beauty of newly fallen snow, or the smell of freshly mown green grass.

Distribute the activity sheet, "Faces and Feelings" and have students draw a face and color it to show how they feel today. Ask them, what would your face look like on Thanksgiving? The first day of school? Other special days?

Share *The Big Orange Splot,* by Daniel Pinkwater. Discuss how Mr. Plumbean takes a stand and paints his house to reflect his individuality.

After sharing some of the stories about painting houses, give each student the activity sheet, "What Color is the Neighborhood." Design a neighborhood where the houses reflect the personalities of the owners.

Draw a simple outline of the house shown in *Oh, Were They Ever Happy!,* by Peter Spier, on a large sheet of paper or a bulletin board. Let the class use watercolors to paint the house just as the Noonan children do in the story.

After sharing *The House That Makes Shapes,* by Jim Potts, give each child an assortment of the five shapes found in the story. Use the shapes to construct a house just as the little boy does in the story.

Divide the class into small groups and ask each group to write another color adventure for Harold. The group may choose to use the purple crayon or to give him a new color. As an alternative, students may choose to feature themselves and a favorite color instead of Harold.

Read *A Winter Walk,* by Lynne Barasch. Brainstorm a list of colors that can be found in winter (or any other season). Talk a walk and discover the colors of the season that surround you. Use watercolors to recreate a favorite scene of a season.

Jane and her brother explore the seashore in *The Paint-Box Sea,* by Doris Herold Lund. After reading the story to the class, discuss how the ocean is constantly changing colors. What other things seem to be in constant change? Ask each student to write a paragraph or poem describing the colors of change in nature, such as the sky, trees, the forest, and the seasons.

Give each student the activity sheet, "Shape

Walk." Explain to the class that they are going to go on a shape walk. As they walk, they need to take notes on the shapes they encounter. Use the activity sheet to draw a map of the walk and some of the shapes and different objects along the way.

Adapt the activity sheet to include a second type of neighborhood walk. Before the walk, have each student choose a shape and/or color from a container. Each child must find objects in the selected shape or color on the walk. Point out the various shades and hues of the colors and the shapes found in familiar objects. Students record their results on the activity sheet along with a map of their walk. If the weather is bad, play the game by walking around the school, house, or library.

Read *Harlequin and the Gift of Colors,* by Remy Charlip and Burton Supree, to the class. Discuss the story of Harlequin, Carnival, Lent, and how Harlequin's friends give up a little of themselves to give Harlequin a lot.

Make a patchwork painting or drawing using a diamond pattern like that in Harlequin's costume. Use scraps of cloth glued to a cardboard design to create a patchwork collage.

In *A Cloak for the Dreamer,* by Aileen Friedman, the three sons create cloaks using geometric shapes. Using the same shapes, have each students design their own cloak using scraps of cloth or colored paper. Draw the cloak outline on paper and glue the scraps in a collage pattern.

Share *The Silly Story of Goldie Locks and the Three Squares,* by Grace Maccarone, with older children. Discuss the pattern of traditional folk tales and how the author integrated shapes into this version of a traditional tale. Write another shape based on another traditional folk tale or nursery rhyme.

Instead of showing the class pictures of Wilbur as a multicolored cat in *Winnie the Witch* by Korky Paul and Valerie Thomas, ask the children draw their version of the colorful cat from the description in the book.

Share *The Great Blueness and Other Predicaments,* by Arnold Lobel. Draw a picture using only black crayons. Paint over the picture with a layer of very thin blue tempera paint to make your own blueness picture.

Nicholas Heller introduces the alphabet and colors in *Goblins in Green.* Use the activity sheet, "Goblins Everywhere," and ask each student to make a list of all the colors from A to Z that the goblins wear. Talk about the different kinds of clothes that the goblins wear and how the colors, names, and types of clothing are keyed into the alphabet.

After sharing *The Ghosts' Dinner* by Jacques Duquennoy, give each student the activity sheet, "Colorful Ghosts," to create their version of a "ghost in flight." Instead of leaving the ghost white, use colored pencils to create colorful characters from the story.

The wacky characters in *Crazy Creatures Colors,* by Hannah Reidy, have a wild and colorful time painting a wall. Sponsor a crazy creature color day and invite the children to wear things that don't match. Talk about the different color combinations. Which colors are worn the most? The least? How many colors were worn? Plan some mismatched activities including painting a mural like the "crazy creatures."

The Frimbles play the "shape" game in *Shopping Spree: Identifying Shapes,* by Monica Weiss. Play the game with the students. Look for shapes and refer to them in "shape" language. Some examples might include: "open the square [window]" or "eat a strawberry ice cream triangle [cone]."

Both *It Looked Like Spilt Milk,* by Charles Shaw, and *Dreams,* by Peter Spier, take a look at shapes found in clouds. Discuss clouds, different types, how they are formed, why and where they happen, and other scientific facts. Go outside and watch the clouds go by. Look for shapes in the clouds and have students discuss what they see. Use dark blue paper and white cotton balls to recreate a shape that is found in the clouds.

Talk about things that change shape like balloons, water, foods, plants, and of course, clouds. Use Play-Doh or clay to create shapes and then redesign the shape.

After sharing *The Chalk Box Story,* by Don Freeman, have the students create a chalk mural. Use a large sheet of butcher paper to create another story about the little boy.

Read *I Want a Blue Banana!,* by Joyce and James Dunbar, to the class. Have the students brainstorm a list of different fruits and vegetables, and compare the list to the ones in the book. Try some different mixtures on the colors for the items named.

Share *Freight Train,* by Donald Crews, with the class. Discuss the different types of cars on the freight train and the loads that they carry. Sing and/or play railroad songs as the children paint large size railroad cars. When finished, display the cars on a bulletin board or wall.

Draw your face and color it based on the way that you feel today. Describe that feeling. What would your face look like on Thanksgiving? The first day of school? What other colors are associated with your feelings on a special day? Draw more faces showing how you look or feel on different occasions.

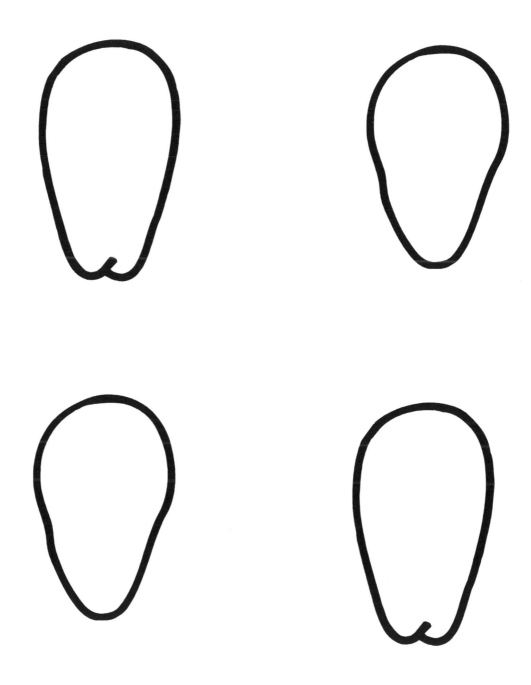

Pretend that all the houses in your neighborhood are painted alike. Everyone decides to change the look of the house. Draw more houses in the neighborhood and paint them to reflect the personalities of their owners.

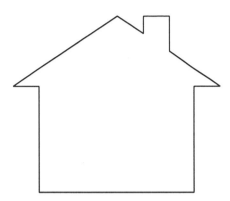

Take a walk around your neighborhood. Use this sheet to draw a map of your course. What shape(s) did your walk take? Make a list of some of the shapes and objects that you saw on the walk.

Goblins Everywhere

The goblins in *Goblins in Green,* by Nicholas Heller, wore all kinds of colorful clothes. Make a list of all the colors and clothes that they tried on and include other colors and garments that they might have found in the attic.

A

B

C

D

E

F

G

H

I

J

K

L

M

N

O

P

Q

R

S

T

U

V

W

X

Y

Z

The ghosts in *The Ghosts' Dinner*, by Jacques Duquennoy, turned the colors of the foods that they ate. Use the ghost pattern to create your version of a "ghost in flight" and make your ghost look like the colorful creatures in the story.

What did your ghost eat to turn him into _____ ghost?

9

ART AND ILLUSTRATION IN COLOR AND SHAPE BOOKS

Art and illustrations are important ingredients in books, and they are especially essential in picture books, especially those that introduce new concepts to young readers. On one hand, the illustrations help explain concepts and show how they relate to a child's familiar world. At the same time, the pictures are creative reflections of an illustrator's imagination and talent in designing unique pieces of art. Illustrators combine a variety of techniques and media such as collage, cut paper, ink, and photographs to convey their visual message to the reader.

Color and shape books look at the topic from the point of view of a particular art form and the artist. Philip Yenawine uses the paintings and sculptures of the New York Museum of Modern Art in his books. *Shapes* and *Colors* show how shapes and colors are very much a part of everyday life. Yenawine is concerned with how children look at art all around them. *Shapes* encourages readers to look beyond the simplistic circle and square to find shapes in everything. Yenawine discusses the visual ideas and effects that can be conveyed by various shapes and how different shapes can elicit a variety of responses. By using real works of art, the author encourages the reader to see that simple shapes are made even more important by placement, precision, and drawing technique. Yenawine uses a similar approach to looking beyond the obvious in *Colors*. Using examples, he isolates the artistic element of color, discusses what thoughts and feelings are evoked by different colors, and examines how color contributes to a work of art. Yenawine looks at color from the artist's point of view, using both representational and abstract paintings to show the effect of color. Yenawine includes notes in the back of each book that give background information on the artists and works of art featured in each book. Both titles look

beyond the simple identification of a shape or color and encourage the reader to think about effects, ideas, and responses to shapes and colors. They are a part of a series designed to help young people learn the basic vocabulary used by artists and would be excellent titles to use with older school students to create deeper discussions about the artistic elements of shape and color.

Museum Colors and *Museum Shapes* are two of the titles in a series by Gisela Voss that combines illustrations of works of art with early concepts. These large-sized board books include a thumb index down the right side of the book that allows the reader to quickly find the color or shape desired. Works from the Boston Museum of Fine Arts, including paintings, sculpture, clothing, and furniture, are used to show a color or shape in these two titles. In *Museum Colors*, the reader is on a scavenger hunt to look at the famous piece of art and find the colored item mentioned in the simple text. A border around each page and the lettering are all in the featured color. A similar page design is used in *Museum Shapes* with a bold, brightly colored border surrounding the text, art, and shape, offset in a contrasting bold color. Ten shapes are introduced with the reader encouraged to find the shape in the featured piece of art. Triangles on a Japanese kimono, stars in a French painting, and squares on a seventeenth-century piece of furniture are a few of the unusual uses of shapes. While background notes on the piece of art and the artist would have been helpful, both of these titles are useful as concept books for beginners and a study in art for older readers.

Shapes and art objects from French culture are the topic of *First Shapes*, by Ivan and Jane Clark Chermayeff. Over fifty objects dating from the Iron Age to the twentieth century are used to show how artists and craftsmen use shapes. Agricultural, culinary, decorative, and religious objects from the Museum National des Arts et Traditions Populaires, including many that are no longer used but have interesting shapes and motifs, are grouped into eighteen shape categories. Color photographs of the real objects are shown against a stark white background. The shapes are identified in English, French, Spanish, German, and Italian and include everything from square, circle, and triangle to star, pinwheel, clover, and spiral. Supplemental material in the back of the book identifies each of the objects used in the main text. *First Shapes* is an excellent title to use to introduce more complex shapes as well as an interesting book for older students in a study of art and real objects.

The final two titles that deal with color and shape from the artist's perspective are *Architecture Colors* and *Architecture Shapes* by Michael J. Crosbie and Steve Rosenthal. While they follow the format of a traditional board book with little text and simple, bold illustrations, both books are very useful in discussing the use of color and shapes in architecture and the architectural elements presented in them. In *Architecture Shapes,* the authors use elements like diamond-shaped window, circular dome, and rectangular windowpanes to show the role of shapes in the construction of various types of buildings. A similar style is used in *Architecture Colors,* with the emphasis on the color of the various elements instead of the shape. Orange bricks, red barn, blue shutters, and a gold dome are a few of the colors presented in this title. Color photographs are used to show the featured shape or color along with a simple one word identification of the shape or color. Both books are part of a series intended to increase interest in architecture and are supported by the National Trust for Historic Preservation.

There are three stories that provide a look at colors and shapes from an artistic viewpoint. In *Color Dance,* by Ann Jonas, several dancers provide a celebration of color and movement. The children use three scarves, one in each of the primary colors, as they slowly dance their way through the pages. As the scarves ebb and flow, they blend and mix together, showing how colors combine to make even more colors. The beautiful watercolor illustrations and simple soothing text offer a look at the color wheel. Colors are also the subject of *Thinking about Colors,* by Jessica Jenkins. When Simon gets a new paint box,

he uses the colors to show different hues and tones of colors. Objects associated with various colors and even moods and feelings are discussed in this unusual book. For example, for the color green, the reader learns about green thumbs, green with envy, sea green, crocodile green, mint green, holly green, and more green things. Finally, there is *Shape Space,* by Cathryn Falwell. A young gymnast opens a box and begins to toss out shapes of all sorts. She dances her way in and around the shapes, arranging and rearranging them into all sorts of objects, including houses, hats, and even a person. The text is filled with rhyme and bounce and accentuates the dance of the gymnast as she plays with shapes. All three of these titles are stories, but with an artistic view of colors and shapes.

One of the most prolific author/illustrators of concept books is Tana Hoban, best known for her unique photographic essays. Hoban uses unusual angles, close-ups, and other techniques to make a reader look at familiar objects in a new light. In one of her earliest books, *Shapes and Things,* photograms of many common objects are used to show shapes. A photogram is a photograph made without a camera. The object is placed directly on photographic paper under darkroom conditions, then exposed to light and processed in the same way as a photographic print. This remarkable wordless book is filled with all sorts of familiar objects grouped loosely together by subject. One page is filled with sewing articles such as lace, thread, pins, needles, and buttons; other pages feature jewelry, tools, and eating utensils. The black-and-white photograms offer a powerful look at shapes and are just as effective today as when they were first published in 1970. In another early book, *Circles, Triangles and Squares,* for which Hoban received an honorable mention for the Children's Science Book Award, she uses black-and-white photographs of ordinary objects to show how these three shapes surround us. Bubbles, hoops, a card house, and rabbits in a cage are a few of the objects shown in this first lesson in basic geometry. Hoban turned to color photographs in some of her later works. *Is It Red? Is It Yellow? Is It Blue? An Adventure in Color* was Hoban's first color photograph book. It concentrates on the primary colors as well as concepts of shapes, quantity and direction. Photographs of common objects (mostly found in cities) fill the pages along with dots across the bottom to show which colors are shown in the photograph. The only text is found on the title pages. In addition to a discussion of colors, this is a good book to use to talk about size, shape and relationships. Children could be encouraged to look in the pictures for answers to questions such as how many wheels are on the red bike, what shape is the jack-o-lantern's eye, and where is the fire hydrant? Hoban has created a visual treat for the reader with an invitation to continue answering the questions in the title. *Dots, Spots, Speckles, and Stripes* takes a look at some unusual shapes found in such common objects as clothing, shells, and sliding boards. The wordless book features color photographs showing colors, shapes, and size relationships in common objects. Like most of Hoban's books, this book looks beyond the obvious and shows more than what meets the eye.

In some ways, *Of Colors and Things* takes a more traditional look at colors in the world. Like many color books, the objects are grouped by color and are displayed in the pictures. Each page is divided into four squares showing various shades of the featured color along with a photograph of a common object. The last object on the page is linked to the first object on the next page. The vibrant photographs of real objects are shown against a stark white background. (Hoban used a black background to show contrast with the color photographs in *Colors Everywhere*.) Next to each photograph are blocks showing which colors are shown in the picture. For example, the photograph of a sunflower includes a yellow block, a tan or light brown one, and an olive green one. Hoban uses brilliant photographs of familiar things including ducks, a parrot, leaves, a jar of jelly beans, and even a basket filled with buttons and threads.

So Many Circles, So Many Squares concentrates on two geometric shapes and how they appear all around us. Using vibrant color photographs and no text, Hoban invites the reader to focus on the circles and squares that can be found in the everyday world. Each page features a single photograph of a familiar object surrounded by a white border. Wheels, signs, pots, grapes, and balloons are a few of the circles and squares of everyday life.

In a slight departure from her usual photographic essays, Hoban has two board books featuring the colors black and white. *Black on White* uses black silhouettes of familiar objects such as butterflies and pails against a white background.

The images are reversed in *White on Black*. White silhouettes of a sailboat, buttons, and even a banana are shown against a black background. Both of these board books are reminiscent of Hoban's early titles using black and white photographs.

In addition to using photographs to illustrate books, artists use a variety of other techniques to convey visual images to the reader. Collage, cut paper, die-cuts, and even paper pulp are some of the different techniques used for illustrations. A collage may use only one type of materials or be composed of several things, including cut-paper designs, paint, and even real materials like cloth or sticks. Leo Lionni uses simple torn paper collage pattern to illustrate his classic story about friendship in *Little Blue and Little Yellow*. He uses an abstract collage design that is simple to grasp and doesn't distract from this powerful tale that explores the theme of judging one another by outward appearances. Little Blue and Little Yellow are best friends who find out that appearances can be deceiving when they accidentally combine to make the color green. This timeless tale originated when Lionni told a story to his two restless grandchildren during a long train ride. It was first published in 1959, but it is still popular today.

Elisa Kleven uses a mixed-media collage in another tale of friendship, *The Lion and the Little Red Bird*. Watercolors, pastels, cut paper, and all kinds of realia (e.g., twigs, fiber, yarn, or grass) are used to create the intricate art in the illustrations. A little bird does his best to try to discover why the lion's tail changes color every day. The bird follows the lion and tries to ask him how the tail changes, but the lion dismisses the chirping bird. While they do not share a spoken language, in the end the two develop a love, respect, and friendship for one another. While colors are not the central focus of this story, color is the common element that creates the friendship between the two creatures.

A mixed media collage is also used in *Brown Cow Green Grass Yellow Mellow Sun,* by Ellen Jackson. The illustrator Victoria Raymond uses a modeling compound called Sculpey to create the brightly colored pictures. A few pieces of fabric, lace, and wire are used to accent the pictures in the book. In this simple cumulative tale, a young boy visits his granny and learns how colors can turn into a special yellow surprise. The modeling clay illustrations are filled with details and are very realistic. Different font sizes and styles are used throughout the text to emphasize the various events that take place. This simple story about the colors of the day and how they unite in a surprise is a good story to share at a storytime for young children.

Cut-paper designs and simple die-cuts are used in *The Color Box,* written by Dayle Ann Dodds and illustrated by Giles Laroche. Each three-dimensional collage scene is filled with cut paper overlays and a die-cut hole. *The Color Box* is the story of Alexander, a curious monkey, who finds an ordinary box with a spot of yellow color inside it. He goes through the spot of color and discovers a world filled with yellow. A small die-cut hole with another color leads Alexander to another colored world. The monkey travels through yellow, orange, blue, red, green, purple, and white until he finally finds a closed door that opens to reveal a world filled with a rainbow of colors. The colored background in each world is filled with cut-paper designs of objects that can be found in the featured color. For example, on the white page, snowmen, snow, and all sorts of white objects fill the page. *The Color Box* is an excellent example of the use of cut-paper designs to create a collage.

Denise Fleming uses an unusual technique to create the illustrations in her contribution to the color book genre, *Lunch.* Instead of paint and brushes, Fleming uses five-gallon buckets of white cotton paper pulp, small squeeze bottles of colored pulp, hand-cut stencils, and a huge wire screen to create "pulp paintings." She begins by dipping the screen in the paper pulp, then pouring colored fiber through the stencils onto the base. The process is repeated several times until many layers of colored pulp are built up. Excess moisture is then removed and the completed image is left to dry for several days. The result is a wonderful story of a very hungry mouse that eats his way through a large, colorful array of foods. The energetic mouse jumps into his meal covering himself with bits and splotches of food, just like a small child. All sorts of familiar foods including "tasty orange carrots," "tart blueberries," and "juicy pink watermelon" fill the pages with bold colors. The minimal text gives a hint about what the mouse will eat next: a small portion of the next food item is shown along the edge of one page and then fully revealed on the next. The mouse eats and eats until his bulging belly can't hold another bite, and then he goes off to

take a nap. Fleming uses very vivid, rich colors that are offset by the contrast of a black-and-white tablecloth in a wonderful frolic through colors and food.

In *Color Farm* and *Color Zoo,* Lois Ehlert uses a cut-out format to create a series of animals who take form as the pages are turned. For example, in *Color Zoo,* a Caldecott Honor book, a triangle, square, and circle are overlaid so that a tiger is transformed into a mouse by the removal of one cut-out shape at a time. The mouse then becomes a fox. The name of the animal appears on the front of each page while the back reveals the name of the shape and a cutout of the shape itself. On the fourth page the three shapes and their names are shown so that the reader can create an original animal. Nine different zoo animals are revealed in the shape die-cutouts. The ten shapes are a star, circle, square, triangle, rectangle, heart, oval, diamond, octagon, and hexagon. Sixteen different shades of colors are also identified in the back of the book. The companion volume, *Color Farm,* uses the same format of a series of animals that take shape as the pages are turned. For example, a rectangle, oval, and triangle are overlaid so that a cat turns into a cow, who in turns becomes a pig by removing one cut-out shape at a time. The name of the animal is revealed on the front page with the identification of the shape on the back of the page. Both books are filled with bold, bright colors, an unusual technique for illustration, and a chance for the reader to touch the die-cut shapes. *Color Zoo* and *Color Farm* provide a tactile as well as a visual exploration of shapes and colors.

A chapter on art would be incomplete without a discussion on the history of color and how colors can be combine to create new tones, hues, and colors. Ariane Dewey offers the reader everything you ever wanted to know about colors in *Naming Colors.* Dewey offers all sorts of quirky, interesting stories about the evolution of words that describe colors. She begins with a brief history of the first words used to describe black, white, and the primary colors and then moves on to trace the history of various hues of colors such as electric pink, Pompeian red, and vermilion. Although the focus of the book is on the history of color language, Dewey offers a great deal of geographic and cultural information as a sidebar. The illustrations are vivid, imaginative, and integrated with the text. Perhaps the best feature of the book is the index, which features color swatches under each color name, making it very easy to look up favorites. *Naming Colors* is a wonderful reference book and a true delight for the artist and etymologist.

Color by Ruth Heller and *The Color Sampler* by Kathleen Westray are two excellent nonfiction titles that discuss the colors and how they are constructed. In *Color,* Ruth Heller uses rhyming text and rich vibrant illustrations to show some very simple facts about colors and to define the concept of commercial color printing. She explains how dots of yellow, magenta, cyan blue, and black are blended to create the illusion of a full spectrum of colors. There are two sections of plastic overlays that show how colors appear when they are overlap. While this book is visually appealing and fun, it does not contain a great deal of information. On the other hand, *The Color Sampler,* by Kathleen Westray, offers a detailcd look at colors, their interaction, and how the human eye perceives colors. Westray uses patchwork quilt patterns to present primary, secondary, intermediate, and complementary colors.

She shows how the color wheel is formed, how the addition of black and white changes colors, and how colors are affected by their placement in a design or by the hues that surround them. The illustrations have been adapted from over two dozen classic patchwork quilt patterns, which are identified at the end of the book. Westray has created a timeless, visually stunning showcase on color concepts.

Art and illustration are a vital part of any book, but they are especially important in books that try to convey basic concepts to the very young and enhance the knowledge of older readers. The pictures are a reflection of the author's and/or illustrator's opinions, imagination, and talent and offer new ways of looking at timeless topics like colors and shapes. Techniques such as photograms, collage, and paper paintings make readers think about colors and shapes in new ways. A picture is truly worth a "thousand words" when it can quickly and easily clarify a concept and make it understood by readers of all ages.

BIBLIOGRAPHY

Colors

Crosbie, Michael J., and Steve Rosenthal. *Architecture Colors*. New York: John Wiley & Sons Inc., 1993. ISBN 0-471-14359-6.

Blue shutters, green roofs, and orange bricks are among the architectural elements that introduce colors.

Dewey, Ariane. *Naming Colors*. New York: HarperCollins, 1995. ISBN 0-06 021292-8; 0-06-021292-6.

Dewey offers a fascinating look at the history and origin of color words in the English language, including primary colors and some distinctive colors, such as sulphur, cypress green, and paprika.

Dodds, Dayle Ann. *The Color Box*. Illustrated by Giles Laroche. Boston, Massachusetts: Little, Brown & Co., 1992. ISBN 0-316-18820-4.

Alexander's curiosity gets the best of him when he discovers an ordinary-looking box with a spot of color.

Fleming, Denise. *Lunch*. New York: Henry Holt and Company, 1992. ISBN 0-8050-1636-8.

A very hungry mouse eats a large, colorful lunch.

Heatwole, Marsha. *Primary Colors*. West Bloomfield, Michigan: Creative Art Press, 1997. ISBN 0-9642712-2-2.

Three primary color cats met, mix, and have some fun.

Heller, Ruth. *Color*. New York: Putnam and Grosset, 1995. ISBN 0-399-22815-2.

Vibrant illustrations, rhyming text, and color overlays are used to introduce some basic principles of color.

Hoban, Tana. *Black on White*. New York: Greenwillow Books, 1993. ISBN 0-688-11918-2.

Black illustrations against a white background show such objects as a butterfly, a pail, and a leaf.

Hoban, Tana. *Colors Everywhere*. New York: Greenwillow Books, 1995. ISBN 0-688-12762-0; 0-688-12763-0 (lib bdg).

Color photographs show how a riot of colors surrounds us.

Hoban, Tana. *Is It Red? Is It Yellow? Is It Blue? An Adventure in Color*. New York: Greenwillow Books, 1978. ISBN 0-688-80171-4; 0-688-84171-6 (lib bdg).

Photographs introduce colors along with shapes, quantity, and direction.

Hoban, Tana. *Of Colors and Things*. New York: Greenwillow Books, 1989. ISBN 0-688-07534-7; 0-688-07535-5 (lib bdg).

Toys, food, and other common objects are grouped according to their colors.

Hoban, Tana. *White on Black*. New York: Greenwillow Books, 1993. ISBN 0-688-11919-0.

White silhouettes against a black background show such objects as a sailboat, buttons, and a banana.

Imershein, Betsy. *Finding Red, Finding Yellow*. New York: Gulliver Books, 1989. ISBN 0-15-200453-X.

Photographs to show the primary colors of red and yellow in the world.

Jackson Ellen. *Brown Cow Green Grass Yellow Mellow Sun*. Illustrated by Victoria Raymond. New York: Hyperion Books for Children, 1995. ISBN 0-7868-0010-0.

When a little boy visits the farm, he discovers that colors can turn into a delicious surprise.

Jenkins, Jessica. *Thinking about Colors*. New York: Dutton Children's Books, 1992. ISBN 0-525-44908-6.

When Simon gets a new paint box, he shows the reader different colors and some of the things associated with each color.

Jeunesse, Gallimard, and Pascale de Bourgoing. *Colors*. Illustrated by P. M. Valet and Sylvaine Perols. New York: Scholastic, Inc., 1989. ISBN 0-590-45236-3.

Yellow and blue combine to make green, red and yellow turn to orange; this book tells the reader more about color.

Jonas, Ann. *Color Dance*. New York: Greenwillow Books, 1989. ISBN 0-688-05990-2; 0-688-05991-0 (lib bdg).

Four dancers show how colors can combine to create more colors.

Jonas, Ann. *Round Trip*. New York: Greenwillow Books, 1983. ISBN 0-688-01772-X; 0-688-01781-9.

Black-and-white illustrations tell about a trip to the city and back home again in the country.

Kleven, Elisa. *The Lion and the Little Red Bird*. New York: Dutton Children's Books, 1992. ISBN 0-525-44898-5.

A little bird tries to find out why the lion's tail changes color everyday.

Lionni, Leo. *Little Blue and Little Yellow*. New York: Astor-Honor, 1959. ISBN 0-8392-3018-4.

Little Blue and Little Yellow are good friends who discover that appearances can be deceiving.

Schroeder, P., and J. Donisch. *Colors*. Vero Beach, Florida: Rourke Publishing Group, 1996. ISBN 0-86625-5818.

Lively rhymes, two-page color photographs, and fun questions introduce the colors of the rainbow.

Voss, Gisela. *Museum Colors*. Boston, Massachusetts: Museum of Fine Arts, 1993. ISBN 0-87846-369-0.
From pink ballerinas by Degas, a blue boat by Homer, and a red bow by Sargent, the reader takes a museum tour of colors.

Westray, Kathleen. *The Color Sampler*. New York: Ticknor & Fields, 1993. ISBN 0-395-65940-X.
Patchwork quilt patterns introduce colors and show how they are affected by what is around them.

Wilson, April. *Magpie Magic: A Tale of Colorful Mischief*. New York: Dial Books, 1999. ISBN 0-8037-73547.
This wordless picture book depicts a young artist who draws a magpie that comes to life.

Yenawine, Philip. *Colors*. New York: Delacorte Press, 1991. ISBN 0-385-30254-1.
Yenawine uses the resources of the Museum of Modern Art to show how artists use colors to create moods and feelings.

Shapes

Chermayeff, Ivan, and Jane Clark Chermayeff. *First Shapes: Premieres Formes Primeras FormasErste Formen Prime Forme*. New York: Harry N. Abrams, Inc., Publishers, 1991. ISBN 0-8109-3819-7.
A collection of French cultural objects dating from the Iron Age to the twentieth century introduces shapes.

Crosbie, Michael J., and Steve Rosenthal. *Architecture Shapes*. Washington, D.C.: The Preservation Press, 1993. ISBN 0-89133-211-1.
Geometric shapes and related architectural elements appear throughout this easy-to-read board book.

Dodds, Dayle Ann. *The Shape of Things*. Illustrated by Julie Lacome. Cambridge, Massachusetts: Candlewick Press, 1994. ISBN 1-56402-224-2.
A shape is just a shape until things are added to it and then it turns into an everyday object.

Falwell, Cathryn. *Shape Space*. New York: Clarion Books, 1992. ISBN 0-395-61305-1.
A young gymnast dances her way around a variety of geometric shapes.

Hoban, Tana. *Circles, Triangles and Squares*. New York: Macmillan Publishing Co., Inc., 1974. ISBN 0-02-744830-4.
Black-and-white photographs show that circles, triangles, and squares are everywhere.

Hoban, Tana. *Dots, Spots, Speckles, and Stripes*. New York: Greenwillow Books, 1987. ISBN 0-688-06862-6; 0-688-06863-4 (lib bdg).
Color photographs show how dots, spots, speckles, and stripes appear in everyday life.

Hoban, Tana. *Shapes and Things*. New York: Macmillan, 1970.
The shapes of many everyday objects appear in this unusual collection of photograms.

Hoban, Tana. *So Many Circles, So Many Squares*. New York: Greenwillow Books, 1998. ISBN 0-688-15165-5; 0-688-15166-3 (lib bdg).
Hoban invites the reader to change the way they look at life by focusing on the circles and squares found in the everyday world.

Voss, Gisela. *Museum Shapes*. Boston, Massachusetts: Museum of Fine Arts, 1993. ISBN 0-87846-368-2.
This memorable board book focuses on shapes in works of art.

Yenawine, Philip. *Shapes*. New York: Museum of Modern Art/Delacorte Press, 1991. ISBN 0-87070-177-0.
This book discusses how artists incorporate shapes in paintings, from simple to geometric to abstract shapes.

Shapes and Colors

Ehlert, Lois. *Color Farm*. New York: J. B. Lippincott, 1990. ISBN 0-397-32440-5; 0-397-32441-3.
Colorful shapes are used to make up all kinds of farm animals.

Ehlert, Lois. *Color Zoo*. New York: J. B. Lippincott, 1989. ISBN 0-397-32259-3; 0-397-32260-7 (lib bdg).
This unique book introduces colors and shapes with zoo animals faces.

ART AND ILLUSTRATION ACTIVITIES

Share with the children books that use paintings and sculpture to demonstrate colors and shapes, and then discuss in detail how the colors and/or shapes in the art affect the children.

Another extension to use with the art books is to discuss the style and content of each work. Identify the artists and find out more about them. Divide the class into small groups and have the groups choose one of the examples used in the books by Gisela Voss or Philip Yenawine or any artist. Find out more about the artist and his/her background and style. Write a brief report about the artist and his or her work.

Take a trip to a local art museum. Give each student the activity sheet, "Colors and Shapes in Works of Art" and have them use the sheet as a guide to locating specific shapes and/or colors. Students can take photographs of their findings. Use the activity sheets and photographs for further discussion after returning to school or home. If a field trip is not feasible, use the Internet and have the student take a virtual trip to a museum. Use this activity with older students and tailor the assignment to the age level of the student.

Divide the class into small groups to create their own "museum" color and/or shape book. Find pictures of paintings, sculpture, or other art objects that clearly show a color or shape. Take a trip to an art museum and take photographs. Use the pictures to create the museum book.

The Chermayeffs use a variety of objects created by artists and craftsmen to show how shapes can be used and expressed in their book, *First Shapes*. With younger children, discuss the shapes that can be found in the objects and then look for shapes in familiar objects such as chairs, tables, utensils, or tools. With older children, discuss the actual objects found in the book (many of them are things that date back to the Iron Age). Have students do some research and report about the objects, their history and uses in society, as well as the shapes that can be found in them. Students can create their own shape book using photographs of real objects such as tools, kitchen utensils, furniture, etc. that is a part of everyday life in the twentieth century. Use the eighteen shape groups used in the book.

While the two books on architectural elements by Michael J. Crosbie and Steve Rosenthal (*Architecture Colors* and *Architecture Shapes*) are designed as board books for young children, they are also useful with older students. Discuss the architectural elements shown in the books. Divide the class into small groups of two to four and send them on a search for pictures to use in creating their own shape or color book based on architecture. Go for a walk and point out some of the elements that were used in the books, as well as others.

After reading *Color Dance* by Ann Jonas, have the students dance to music using scarves in the three primary colors. Watch how the colors blend and flow together to create new colors.

Before sharing *Thinking about Colors* by Jessica Jenkins, hold a brainstorming session about colors. Choose a color and brainstorm a list of phrases, moods, and objects associated with the color. Another activity is to have each child choose a color and write a paragraph or two telling the phrase, moods, feelings, and objects associated with that color.

After looking at *Shapes and Things,* by Tana Hoban, ask each child to make a photogram. Each student chooses a theme (office supplies, kitchen utensil, toys, etc.) for the photogram. If a darkroom is available, place the objects directly on photographic paper, expose them to light, and process like any photographic print. If a darkroom is not available, then the children can trace or draw the shapes on white paper and glue on a black background.

Create your own color-coded photograph book based on *Is It Red? Is It Yellow? Is It Blue?* by Tana Hoban. Take your own pictures or cut out pictures from magazines for the main text. Mount the pictures on white paper and include color dots of all the shades used in the picture. For older students, write a paragraph or two exploring some of the things in the photograph such as shape, perception, size, etc.

Share a red, yellow, and blue snack such as blue gelatin with slices of yellow and red apples.

After discussing *Dots, Spots, Speckles, and Stripes* by Tana Hoban, make a game of trying to find more of these shapes around us. Try to find at least two examples of each of the four items.

Show the examples used in *Circles, Triangles and Squares* by Tana Hoban. Divide the children into pairs or let them work individually and have them take photographs of at least six basic shapes. The photographs must be of ordinary objects with only one shape per object. Mount the pictures on colorful backgrounds and display them.

Tana Hoban uses the idea of silhouettes in one color against a contrasting back in the board books *White on Black* and *Black on White*. Choose two constrasting colors (e.g., yellow and purple or red and white) to create a color book of familiar objects.

Discuss what happens to the two friends in *Little Blue and Little Yellow,* by Leo Lionni. Talk about friendship and appearances. Discuss how blue and yellow combine to create a third color. What would have happened if Little Blue or Little Yellow had met Little Red? Write another story about Little Blue and his friends.

Write another adventure or scene for the bird and lion from Elisa Kleven's *The Lion and the Little Red Bird.* Create your own mixed media collage of the scene.

The little boy is treated to a yummy surprise in *Brown Cow Green Grass Yellow Mellow Sun,* by Ellen Jackson. Make your own delicious snack by using the pancake and butter recipes included in the back of the book.

Use modeling clay to create a picture like those in *Brown Cow Green Grass Yellow Mellow Sun.* Add bits of grass, fabric, sticks, or some other realia to make the collage more realistic looking.

Create a color collage using only materials in one color. For example, if you choose the color red, then use things like red beans, red sparkles, scraps of red paper, red yarn, and red sequins to make the collage.

After sharing *Lunch,* by Denise Fleming, discuss the art of papermaking. Describe how Fleming creates her illustrations from cotton fiber. Show the process to the children by either showing the video of Denise Fleming that is available from the publisher, Henry Holt, or by using her papermaking kit available from bookstores. You can also soak white paper in water to show what paper fiber looks like.

Carefully examine the illustrations *Color Zoo* and *Color Farm* by Lois Ehlert. Discuss the use of different shapes used to form the animals and the use of the bold, bright colors in the simple designs. Using the same pattern of Lois Ehlert, have each student create a series of three pictures using overlay cut-out shapes to form the image. Be sure to use a simple image or animals to create a series of three images transformed by the turning of the page.

Give each child an activity sheet to use to create his or her own "Colorful Shape Animal." Use only three shapes and three colors to create an animal like those in the books by Lois Ehlert.

Let the children experiment with colors by using tempera paint and sponges. Dip the sponges into the paint and lightly press onto paint. Experiment with designs and watch what happens when colors overlap to create even more colors.

Give each child a handful of colorful circles from a paper punch. Use the small circles to create a mosaic or collage picture of a round object. Use one-inch squares or small triangles to create a mosaic of square or triangle objects.

After discussing colors, have the students plan a redecorating project. Go to a local paint store and get paint charts or color strips. Make a chart to record and compare answers about color changes such as repainting the family car, choosing new carpet for the classroom, changing the color of your hair, or repapering the dining room.

Use Ariane Dewy's *Naming Colors* as a guide to finding out more about color words. Divide the class into small groups and assign each group a color to research. Brainstorm a list of shades and hues of each color before starting. Then find out more about the color and its many hues and tones.

The Color Sampler, by Kathleen Westray, is an excellent title to use with older students, especially those in middle and high school. Talk about the use of color to create a variety of effects in the patchwork quilts and in other places. Use color shapes to recreate some of the patterns in the book. For older students, have them research the quilt patterns used in the book. Find out more about their history and origins. Using some of the color principles that Westray discusses, create a quilt mural.

Colors and Shapes in Works of Art

Take a trip to a local art museum. Find examples of the following colors
 and shapes in works of art including paintings, sculpture, furniture, etc.
Use the sample card at the bottom to record information about each art object that you view.

Circle: Red:

Square: Yellow:

Triangle: Blue:

Rectangle: Green:

Oval: Purple:

Star: Orange:

Diamond: Pink:

Crescent: White:

Heart: Black:

Arrow:

Spiral:

For each shape or color that you find record the following information:

Name of Work and Artist:

Type of art:

Materials used:

Date of artwork:

Notes:

Colorful Shape Animals

Use no more than three shapes and three colors to create a simple shape animal like those found in *Color Zoo* and *Color Farm,* by Lois Ehlert. You may use shapes other than those shown.

10

COLORS, SHAPES, AND MORE

The books in this chapter fit into two categories: beginning books and pop culture. Board books have already been discussed, but there are many books that introduce the idea of colors or shapes in the form of a beginning reader. The text is usually more complex than that of a board book and is designed for preschool and primary students. The second category concentrates on concept books that feature well-known characters from books, television, and movies.

Robert J. Wolff has a series of titles featuring one color. Each of the books (*Feeling Blue, Hello Yellow!* and *Seeing Red*), describes the characteristics of the featured color, qualities of the various shades of the color, how it can be combined to form new colors, and things associated with the featured color. The pages are filled with varying shades of the featured color. Although Wolff's series was published in 1968, these three titles are still useful today.

Using color photographs against a stark white background has become a popular trend in books during the past few years. *My First Look at Colors* and *My First Look at Shapes* are two such volumes. The pages are packed with vivid closeup photographs of everyday objects such as red boots, blue mittens, and pink ballet slippers. Both of these titles show how colors and shapes affect every aspect of our lives. In a similar vein, Debbie MacKinnon and Neil Ricklen use photographs of children exploring their worlds and discovering shapes and colors. In *Colors: A First Word Book*, Ricklen shows children playing with all sorts of familiar objects in the featured color. The text includes big, bold letters identifying the color as well as smaller text identifying all the objects in the photographs. A group of happy, curious toddlers explores the world and discovers a variety of shapes in *What Shape?* by Debbie MacKinnon. On the left is a question about

shapes, while the facing page shows photographs of everyday objects in the featured shape.

Colors around Us, by Shelley Rotner and Anne Woodhull, also uses photographs of familiar things to show colors but adds a little extra twist with rhymes and flaps to lift. From end sheet to end sheet, the pages are filled with rich color photographs of familiar objects in all the colors of the rainbow. A die-cut stencil of the color word invites the reader to lift the word flap and discover the colorful object underneath. A second flap for each color spread poses a color rhyme that can only be answered by looking beneath the flap. For example, on the blue page, the rhyme states that "blue floats," while under the flap, the reader discovers a blue boat floating in a sea of blue water. Each color spread includes a variety of hues and simple text that identifies the objects in each photograph. The vivid color photographs are printed on heavy cardstock and include four to eight objects per color. *Colors around Us* is useful as a simple introduction to colors for young children or as an example of photographic essays for older children.

Children are featured in the illustrations in *If You Take a Paintbrush* by Fulvio Testa. A simple sentence on the left describes the action, while the facing page is an illustration illuminating a single color. Children are shown in all sorts of ordinary scenes with colors surrounding them. Crisp white snow under a sled, oranges falling from a tree, and a swing hanging from a green limb are only a few of the color objects in Testa's rich drawings.

John J. Reiss covers both colors and shapes in his contributions to the concept genre. In *Colors,* each color page shows things to eat, wear, chase, and pat in the bright vibrant drawings. The author invites reader participation in identifying all of the familiar things for each color. *Colors* is one of the few books about color that shows the various shades of a color. The green pages show a frog in several shades of green, a pale green snake coiling through darker green grass, and several leaf shapes in a variety of greens. He uses the same type of advanced thinking in *Shapes.* Reiss goes beyond the simple identification of familiar shapes by providing a look at how simple shapes evolve into more complex shapes: squares become cubes, triangles become pyramids, circles make spheres. He shows the reader how rectangles, ovals, pentagons, and hexagons are found in a variety of objects from musical notes to bricks. Brightly colored backgrounds and comical animal characters that juggle, skate, and dance across the pages show that shapes are all around us.

Ed Emberley is well known for his books on drawing, and he uses his talents to show the role of colors and shapes in the world in two nonfiction titles. In *Green Says No,* Emberley tackles the topic of colors: how colors are made, what happens when they are mixed, and how to get dark and light colors are all discussed. Throughout the text, Emberley reminds the reader about some of the things that colors mean. For example, orange and black stand for Halloween, blue signifies sadness, and red often means embarrassment. In *The Wing on a Flea: A Book about Shapes,* Emberley concentrates on three shapes (circle, triangle, rectangle) with the featured shape highlighted in color in the black and white line drawings. Emberley offers a simple but effective way to encourage the reader to "just look and see," shapes are all around.

Characters from books, cartoons, television programs, and even feature films are often used to introduce concepts while telling stories. The famous Hundred Acre Wood is the scene of *Winnie the Pooh's Colors,* by Ernest H. Shepard, one volume in a series on various concepts that uses A. A. Milne's famous characters. The Hundred Acre Wood is a colorful place to visit and see gray Eeyore, orange Tigger, and all the friends of that golden bear, Winnie the Pooh. This book uses images from the classic stories, recalling items like Pooh's blue balloon, Christopher Robin's green door, and even Pooh's red sweater to introduce colors. A simple sentence with the color highlighted describes the illustrations. Winnie the Pooh and his friends are as popular today as when they were first introduced. Characters from the classic tales by Beatrix Potter are the subject of a board book series on early concepts. In *Learn with Jemina Puddle-Duck,* Jemina Puddle-Duck searches for a new house. As she looks, she finds all kinds of shapes including a rectangle door, square window, and triangle roof. Finally, she finds the perfect place to hatch her brand new oval egg. Benjamin Bunny, along with other classic Potter characters, introduces colors in *Benjamin Bunny's Colors.* Both of these board books use simple sentences and illustrations from the classic Beatrix Potter stories to introduce concepts.

Two other classic book characters, Babar and Paddington Bear, have their own color books. In *Babar's Book of Color,* by Laurent de Brunhoff, Babar lets his three children play in his studio. Like all curious children, they soon tire of simply painting and begin to experiment and mix colors. The bold, bright illustrations and the pleasant story line help the reader learn more about mixing and using colors. In *Paddington's Colors,* Paddington Bear decides to do his spring cleaning, and in the process he finds all sorts of colorful things. Paddington does ordinary chores like painting, wallpapering, and even washing his clothes. The only text in the main body of the book is an identification of the color, but in the back the reader is asked to name all the colors of the rainbow.

The popular pooch Spot introduces shapes and colors in two board books and a larger oversized book for older readers. In *Spot Looks at Colors* and *Spot Looks at Shapes,* Spot and his friends frolic and discover colors and shapes all around them. The text is a simple sentence describing Spot and whatever he happens to be doing. In the oversized volume, *Spot's Big Book of Colors, Shapes, and Numbers,* by Eric Hill, Spot and his buddies have fun with concepts of all sorts. The color and shape sections feature is a simple identification of objects along with questions asking the reader to find things on the pages.

Lowly Worm, Huckle Cat, Mr. Paint Pig, and other characters from Busytown can be found in several books about shapes and colors. The lovable characters of Richard Scarry tell all in *Colors.* Small paint buckets at the tops of the pages show the featured color plus many shades of the color (blue, dark blue, light blue, etc.). In addition to introducing basic colors and shades, Scarry includes information about mixing colors and creating new colors. *Colors* and *Shapes and Opposites* are part of a series, First Little Learners. Only a small section of *Shapes and Opposites* deals with shapes, but it includes all the basic ones (e.g., circle, star, triangle, and square) and some examples of objects that are made up of the shapes. Stark white backgrounds and bright, colorful cartoon characters fill the pages along with more text than is usually found in beginning readers. In typical Scarry style, the pages are filled with busy scenes with all the familiar animals engaged in a variety of activities. Mr. Paint Pig is the central character in *Richard Scarry's Colors* and *Richard Scarry's Pop-Up Colors*. Both titles have a similar plot with Mr. Paint Pig busily painting all over Busytown. Many of the familiar Scarry characters such as Hilda Hippo, Huckle Cat, and Bananas Gorilla are a part of stories to introduce colors. Clever pop-ups and pull tabs are used throughout the second title to help make learning fun. In *Huckle Cat's Colors,* Huckle shows the readers all the colors found in Busytown such as a green pickle car and a yellow bananamobile. With a little help from his Busytown friends, Lowly Worm bends and forms all sorts of shapes in *Lowly Worm's Shapes and Sizes.* Both of these board books are sure to delight young children.

Thomas the Tank Engine is another classic book character who has his own shape and color books. In *Thomas the Tank Engine Colors* and *Thomas the Tank Engine Shapes and Sizes,* Thomas chugs his way across the pages. He meets friends like Bertie the Bus and Harold the Helicopter as they show off colors and shapes. Both of these titles are board books.

Television and cartoons are fertile fields for teaching children all about basic concepts and other ideas. As an extension of such programs as *Sesame Street* and *Barney,* the creators of the programs issue books that feature one or more of the characters from the series as they talk about colors, shapes, or some other topic for young learners. Many of the characters from *Sesame Street* are a part of *Big Bird Is Yellow: A Sesame Street Book of Colors.* Big Bird, Oscar, Bert and the other characters invite the reader to look for a specific color item on the pages. Bold, colorful photographs fill the pages of this title. Baby Grover is the central character in *Little Grover's Book of Shapes* by Anna Ross. On one side of the page, Little Grover is asked a question about a shape. On the facing page, he must find the shape in everyday objects that surround him such as ovals in Big Bird's mirror, Oscar's grapes, and

ordinary white eggs. While Big Bird searches his bag for something red in *Big Bird's Red Book,* by Rosanne and Jonathan Cerf, all sorts of red objects (fire engines, birds, Santa, and more) appear around him. The text is in cartoon balloons, enhancing the humorous mood of the tale. Finally, Big Bird finds red when he sits down on a bag of red tomatoes. Although only one color is featured, Big Bird and his friends do an excellent job of discussing red.

Barney and his friends also have several board books that deal with basic concepts. In *Baby Bop Discovers Shapes* by Stephen White, Baby Bop invites the reader to help her find shapes on the pages. Die-cuts are an integral part of the illustrations that help even the youngest reader to quickly find the shape on the page. Simple rhyming couplets and colorful pictures are used throughout this larger-sized board book. Even though the popular Baby Bop is featured, the emphasis is on finding the shape and how it looks in ordinary objects. The big purple dinosaur, Barney, uses his paint set to color objects in *Barney's Color Surprise* by Mary Ann Dudko. The illustrations are a combination of photographs and drawings along with rhyming couplets. Along with the paint box and identification of the color, four familiar items for each color are used in this board book.

Feature films, especially Disney films, offer ample opportunities to use popular characters to introduce concepts like colors and shapes. Simba, Dumbo, Mickey, and even Pocahontas join other Disney characters in showing how colors and shapes are important elements in the world. In *Disney's Pop-Up Book of Shapes,* Mickey and the gang discover the magic and fun of shapes. Mickey performs magic tricks using shapes such as circle, squares, and triangles. Other Disney characters (e.g., Goofy, Minnie, Pluto, etc.) join the fun as shapes pop up on the pages. In a first "Golden" book, *Walt Disney's Dumbo's Book of Colors,* Dumbo tries to find a colorful gift for his friend Timothy Mouse. As Dumbo searches high and low for the perfect color to cheer up his friend, he helps the other circus performers as well. Finally Dumbo discovers that a bouquet of balloons does the trick and makes Timothy a star. One of the more unusual concept books using Disney characters is *Lunch Bugs: Simba's Book about Colors.* In this touch-and-play book, Timon and Pumba invite Simba to join them for a colorful feast. One by one, Timon and Pumba tell Simba about each of the colorful bugs that they prefer to eat. They describe the taste and texture of each delicious bug. Die-cut bug shapes on the cover and throughout the book are used to reveal the touchable bugs. Vibrant illustrations re-create the popular characters from *The Lion King* along with the irresistibly touchable bugs that poke through the pages. Based on the animated Disney film, *Disney's Pocahontas, Painting with the Wind: A Book about Color,* by Teddy Slater, not only introduces colors but also provides a message about nature. Pocahontas leads John Smith through the forest, helping him to see the colors of nature and the beauty of her world. The lush full-color illustrations hold true to the film images and are accompanied by a gentle, soothing text. A wide stenciled border of leaves across the bottom of each double-page spread is in the color featured in the text and illustration.

Although this book is clearly a commercial tie-in to the Disney film, it is a wonderful title to use with a discussion on the colors of nature. From a trail of yellow leaves floating past a brown log to fragrant pink flowers where Flit looks for nectar, Slater has created a celebration of colors and nature.

Many beginner books feature photographs and simple illustrations to show readers how colors and shapes are all around us. While these books are usually designed for preschoolers and beginning readers, they are also useful with older students as examples of books that clearly get the information across to the reader. In addition to beautiful photo essays, beginner books feature familiar characters from literature, television, and even feature films. Because these characters are already familiar and comforting to readers, they are effective tools to use in presenting information and introducing basic concepts.

BIBLIOGRAPHY

Colors

Baker, Piers. *Matching Colors*. New York: Little Simon, 1997. ISBN 0-689-81568-9.
Crisp photographs and hands-on activities help young readers learn about colors.

Balducci, Rita. *Walt Disney's Alice in Wonderland*. Illustrated by Sue DiCicco. Racine, Wisconsin: Western Publishing Company, 1993. ISBN 0-307-06079-9.
Alice and her friends from Wonderland introduce colors.

Benjamin Bunny's Colors. Middlesex, England: Frederick Warne & Co., 1993. ISBN 0-7232-4118-X.
Benjamin Bunny and other Beatrix Potter characters tell all about colors.

Big Bird Is Yellow: A Sesame Street Book of Colors. Photographs by John E. Barrett. New York: Random House/Children's Television Workshop, 1990. ISBN 0-679-80752-7.
Big Bird and other Sesame Street characters invite the reader to find things in different colors.

Bond, Michael. *Paddington's Colors*. Illustrated by John Lobban. New York: Viking, 1990. ISBN 0-670-84102-1.
As Paddington Bear does his spring cleaning, he discovers that colors can be fun.

Bragg, Ruth Gembicki. *Colors of the Day*. Saxonville, Massachusetts: Picture Book Studios, 1992. ISBN 0-88708-245-9.
A little girl sees a color wheel in a summer day.

Brown, Marc. *D.W.'s Color Book*. New York: Random House, 1997. ISBN 0-679-88439-4.
Lift-the-flaps and join D.W. on a fun-filled springtime egg hunt in this colorful board book.

Brunhoff, Laurent de. *Babar's Book of Color*. New York: Random House, 1984. ISBN 0-394-86896-X.
Babar lets his three children visit his studio and play with his paints.

Burningham, John. *John Burningham's Colors*. New York: Crown Publishers, Inc., 1985. ISBN 0-517-55961-7.
A little boy leads the reader through the world of colors with such familiar things as yellow balloons, purple grapes, and white snow.

Cerf, Rosanne, and Jonathan Cerf. *Big Bird's Red Book*. Illustrated by Michael J. Smollin. Wayne, New Jersey: Golden Press, 1971. ISBN 0-307-60157-9.
While Big Bird searches for something red, he is unaware of all the red things around him.

Chermayeff, Ivan. *Tomato and Other Colors*. Englewood Cliffs, New Jersey: Prentice-Hall, 1980. ISBN 0-13-924753-X.
Color conveys many different messages.

Colors with Dib, Dab, and Dob. New York: DK Publishing, Inc., 1998. ISNB 0-7894-2912-8.
Three little ducks, Dib, Dab, and Dob, introduce colors.

Come and See with Dipsy. New York: Scholastic, 1999. ISBN 0-590-38625-5. This foldout book reveals Dipsy, from *Teletubbies*, and his book of green objects.

Come and See with Laa Laa. New York: Scholastic, 1999. ISBN 0-590-38626-3.
Laa Laa, from *Teletubbies*, shares all sorts of yellow objects.

Come and See with Po. New York: Scholastic, 1999. ISBN 0-590-38627-1.
Po, from *Teletubbies*, tells all about red things with a series of photographs in this fold-out board book.

Come and See with Tinky Winky. New York: Scholastic, 1999. ISBN 0-590-38624-7.
Tinky Winky, from *Teletubbies*, shows purple objects in this board book.

Cousins, Lucy. *Maisy's Colors*. Cambridge, Massachusetts: Candlewick Press, 1997. ISBN 0-7636-0237-X.
Maisy shows off her colorful toys, clothes, and other objects in an oversized board book.

Disney's Pop-Up Book of Colors. Los Angeles, California: Disney Press, 1991. ISBN 1-56282-020-6.
Mickey, Donald, and the gang explore the world of colors.

Dudko, Mary Ann. *Barney's Color Surprise*. Illustrated by Margie Larsen; photographs by Dennis Full. Allen, Texas: Barney Publications, 1993. ISBN 1-57064-007-6.
Barney uses his paint set to color everyday objects.

Emberley, Ed. *Green Says No*. Boston, Massachusetts: Little Brown & Co., 1968. ISBN 0-316-23599-7.
This readable fact book discusses colors, how they are made, what happens when they are mixed, and how to get dark and light colors.

Gaudrat, Marie-Agnes, and Thierry Courtin. *Discover Colors*. Adapted by Judith Herbst. Hauppauge, New York: Barron's Educational Series, Inc., 1994. ISBN 0-8120-6497-6.
Humorous animal characters introduce colors, show different hues, and even demonstrate how colors work together and against each other.

Gordon, Maria. *Fun with Colors*. Illustrated by Mike Gordon. New York: Thomson Learning, 1995. ISBN 1-56847-439-3; 1-56847-501-2 (pbk).
Amazing facts and fun activities are presented in this beginning book of colors.

Gundersheimer, Karen. *Colors to Know*. New York: Harper & Row, Publishers, 1986. ISBN 0-694-00066-3; 0-06-022196-8 (lib bdg).
When a teeny tiny girl goes exploring, she discovers color all around her.

Hill, Eric. *Spot Looks at Colors*. New York: G. P. Putnam's Sons, 1986. ISBN 0-399-21349-X.
As Spot plays, he finds many colorful objects.

Inkpen, Mick. *Kipper's Book of Colors*. San Diego, California: Red Wagon Books/ Harcourt Brace & Company, 1994. ISBN 0-15-200647-8.
That tiny dog Kipper shows colors found in common objects.

Konigsburg, E. L. *Samuel Todd's Book of Great Colors*. New York: Atheneum, 1990. ISBN 0-689-31593-7.
Simple text and bold, bright illustrations introduce colors and where they can be found.

Lunch Bugs: Simba's Book about Colors. Los Angeles, California: Mouseworks, 1995. ISBN 1-57082-125-9.
Timon and Pumba show Simba some irresistible but colorful bugs.

Miller, J. P., and Katherine Howard. *Do You Know Colors?* New York: Random House, 1978. ISBN 0-394-83957-9; 0-394-93957-3 (lib bdg).
A parrot artist reveals colors and how they blend to make more colors.

My First Look at Colors. New York: Random House, 1990. ISBN 0-679-80535-4.
Photographs of such real objects as red boots, blue mittens, pink ballet slippers, and white chalk introduce the concept of color.

Pashuk, Lauren. *Fun with Colors*. Milwaukee, Wisconsin: Penworthy Publishing Co., 1985. ISBN 0-87617-028-9.
A host of happy children look for colors all around them.

Price, Sarah. *The Poky Little Puppy's Book of Colors*. Illustrated by Sarah Chandler. Racine, Wisconsin: Western Publishing Company, Inc., 1995. ISBN 0-307-12725-7.
As he plays, the Poky Little Puppy discovers colors everywhere.

Red Bug, Blue Bug. Mouseworks, 1998. ISBN 1-57082-992-6.
The silly circus bugs from *A Bug's Life* show off their colors.

Reiss, John J. *Colors*. Scarsdale, New York: Bradbury Press, 1969. ISBN 0-87888-008-9.
This vibrant introduction to colors showcases things to eat, wear, chase, and pat.

Reit, Seymour. *Adventures with Color*. Pictures by J. P. Miller. New York: Western Publishing Co., 1963, 1970.
This title describes how and when colors are helpful.

Ricklen, Neil. *Colors: A First Word Book*. New York: Little Simon, 1994. ISBN 0-671-86726-1.
Photographs of children teach colors and first words simultaneously.

Ross, Anna. *Little Elmo's Book of Colors*. Illustrated by Norman Gorbaty. New York: Random House, 1992. ISBN 0-679-82238-0.
Little Elmo tells about the colors that he needs to paint a picture.

Rotner, Shelley, and Anne Woodhull. *Colors around Us*. Photographs by Shelley Rotner. New York: Little Simon, 1996. ISBN 0-689-80980-8.
Sunny images and playful rhymes emphasize the colors around us.

Scarry, Richard. *Colors*. New York: J. B. Communications, Inc., 1995. ISBN 1-56144-722-6.
Huckle Cat, Lowly Worm, and other friends from Busytown introduce colors.

Scarry, Richard. *Huckle Cat's Colors*. New York: Simon and Schuster, 1998. ISBN 0-689-81655-3.
Huckle shows colors around Busytown.

Scarry, Richard. *Richard Scarry's Colors*. New York: Golden Press, 1992. ISBN 0-307-67542-4.
Paint Pig loves colors so much that he paints everything in sight.

Scarry, Richard. *Richard Scarry's Pop-Up Colors*. New York: Little Simon, 1996. ISBN 0-689-80330-3.
Mr. Paint Pig paints his world all different colors.

Schulz, Charles M. *Snoopy's Book of Colors*. Racine, Wisconsin: Western Publishing Co., Inc., 1987. ISBN 0-307-10929-1; 0-307-60929-4 (lib bdg).
Snoopy and other Peanuts characters find colors in all kinds of everyday items.

Seah, Jeffrey. *Colours*. Singapore: Mighty Minds Corporation, 1993. ISBN 0-981-3021-45-4.
Photographs are used in this basic introduction to colors.

Seah, Jeffrey. *Colours*. Illustrated by Alain Fontaine. Singapore: Mighty Minds Corporation, 1994. ISBN 0-981-3053-54-2.
Amusing characters in unusual situations, such as angels playing tennis, introduce colors.

Shepard, Ernest H. *Winnie the Pooh's Colors*. New York: Dutton, 1995. ISBN 0-525-45428-4.
The Hundred Acre Wood is a colorful place to visit with gray Eeyore, orange Tigger, golden bear Winnie the Pooh, and his friends.

Sieveking, Anthea. *What Color?* New York: Dial Books for Young Readers, 1990. ISBN 0-8037-0909-9.
Color photos and brief text display a variety of objects that are familiar to babies.

Slater, Teddy. *Disney's Pocahontas, Painting with the Wind: A Book about Color*. Illustrated by Ed Ghertner and Del Thompson. Los Angeles, California: Disney Press, 1995. ISBN 0-7868-3041-7; 0-7868-5031-0 (lib bdg).
As Pocahontas wanders through the forest, she looks at the beauty and colors of nature.

Steiner, Charlotte. *My Slippers Are Red*. New York: Alfred A. Knopf, 1957.
Rhyming text helps the reader learn about different colors.

Testa, Fulvio. *If You Take a Paintbrush: A Book of Colors*. New York: The Dial Press, 1982. ISBN 0-8037-3829-3.
Scenes of children playing show off colors.

Thomas the Tank Engine Colors. Illustrated by Pam Posey. New York: Random House, 1991. ISBN 0-679-81646-1.
Thomas and his friends show off their colors in this sturdy board book.

Tiny Toon Adventures First Book of Colors. New York: Heinemann, 1992. ISBN 0-434-96043-8.
As the Tiny Toon characters work and play, they display a variety of colors.

Turner, Gwenda. *Colors*. New York: Viking Kestrel, 1989. ISBN 0-670-82552-2.
Children's face paintings introduce colors.

Vischer, Phil. *Junior's Colors*. Nashville, Tennessee: Tommy Nelson, Inc., 1997. ISBN 0-8499-1487-6.
Junior Asparagus and Bob the Tomato introduce colors using common items.

Walt Disney's Dumbo's Book of Colors. Racine, Wisconsin: Western Publishing Company, Inc., 1988. ISBN 0-307-10170-3.
When his friend Timothy Mouse is sad, Dumbo decides to give him a colorful gift to cheer him up.

Walt Disney Productions Presents Goofy's Book of Colors. New York: Random House, 1983. ISBN 0-394-95734-2.
Goofy and his Disney friends learn about colors.

Weiss, Ellen. *Baby Kermit's Color Book*. Illustrated by Lauren Attinello. Racine, Wisconsin: Western Publishing Co., 1993. ISBN 0-307-12539-4.
Baby Kermit and his friends introduce thirteen familiar colors.

Williams, Rozanne Lanczak. *I See Colors*. Photographs by Keith Bergher. Cypress, California: Creative Teaching Press, 1994. ISBN 0-916119-32-7.
The reader learns about colors from photographs of colorful objects.

Wolff, Robert Jay. *Feeling Blue*. New York: Charles Scribner's Sons, 1968. ISBN 0-684-12528-5.
Wolff explores the hows and whys of the color blue.

Wolff, Robert Jay. *Hello Yellow!* New York: Charles Scribner's Sons, Scribner, 1968.
Children explore yellow's relationship to orange, green, red, and blue.

Wolff, Robert Jay. *Seeing Red*. New York: Charles Scribner's Sons, 1968.
The author paints a picture story of the color red and all that it can be.

Shapes

Baby Mickey's Book of Shapes. Racine, Wisconsin: Western Publishing Co., 1986. ISBN 0-307-10165-7.
While looking everywhere for his favorite toy, Baby Mickey encounters all sorts of shapes.

Baker, Piers. *Matching Shapes*. New York: Little Simon, 1997. ISBN 0-689-81569-7.
Match, sort, and identify the images on a cube to those in the book in this easy book about shapes.

Bernthal, Mark S. *Barney's Book of Shapes*. Illustrated by Darren McKee. Allen, Texas: Barney Pub., 1998. ISBN 1-57064-242-7,
Barney finds all sorts of shapes when he goes for a walk.

Disney's Pop-Up Book of Shapes. Los Angeles, California: Disney Press, 1991. ISBN 1-56282-019-2.
Mickey and the gang discover the magic and fun of shapes.

Emberley, Ed. *The Wing on a Flea: A Book about Shapes*. Boston, Massachusetts: Little, Brown & Co., 1961.
Shapes are all around us.

Fries, Marcia. *I See Shapes*. Cypress, California: Creative Teaching Press, 1995. ISBN 0-916119-86-8.
In this simple story, familiar shapes turn into all sorts of objects: triangles become party hats, circles become balloons, and squares become presents.

Gave, Marc. *Walt Disney's Pinocchio Fun with Shapes and Sizes*. Illustrated by John Kurtz. New York: Golden Press, 1992. ISBN 0-307-12332-4.
Pinocchio and his friends introduce shapes and sizes.

Gillham, Bill, and Susan Hulme. *Let's Look at Shapes*. Photographs by Jan Siegieda. New York: Coward-McCann, Inc., 1984. ISBN 0-698-20615-0.
Children look for shapes in the world around them.

Gundersheimer, Karen. *Shapes to Know*. New York: Harper & Row, Publishers, 1986. ISBN 0-694-00067-1.
As Memo and Minna Mouse play with their toys, they learn about different shapes.

Hefter, Richard. *The Strawberry Book of Shapes*. New York: Strawberry Books, 1976. ISBN 0-88470-021-6.
Bears of all sorts introduce all sorts of shapes.

Hill, Eric. *Spot Looks at Shapes*. New York: G. P. Putnam's Sons, 1986. ISBN 0-399-21350-3.

Popular pooch Spot shows off the different shapes in our world.

Hughes, Shirley. *All Shapes and Sizes.* New York: Lothrop, Lee and Shepard Books, 1986. ISBN 0-688-04205-8.
Rhyming text describes the different shapes and sizes of ordinary things.

Learn with Jemima Puddle-Duck: A Book of Shapes. Avenel, New Jersey: Derrydale Books, 1993. ISBN 0-517-07699-3.
Jemima Puddle-Duck searches for a new house with just the right shapes.

MacKinnon, Debbie. *What Shape?* Photographs by Anthea Sieveking. New York: Dial Books, 1992. ISBN 0-8037-1244-8.
A group of happy, curious toddlers explore the world and find plenty of shapes.

My First Look at Shapes. New York: Random House, 1990. ISBN 0-679-80534-6.
Colorful photographs of simple objects help the reader explore the concept of shapes, such as diamonds, stars, and circles.

Namm, Diane. *My First Book of Shapes.* Illustrated by Wayne Becker. New York: Checkerboard Press, 1987, 1992.
When Little Circle searches for someone to roll along with him, he makes a new friend.

Peppe, Rodney. *The Shapes Finder.* New York: Bedrick/Blackie, 1991. ISBN 0-87226-462-9.
This oversized board book introduces simple shapes.

Pragoff, Fiona. *Shapes.* New York: Doubleday, 1989. ISBN 0-385-26408-9.
As a little girl plays, she discovers that her toys come in many shapes.

Reiss, John J. *Shapes.* Scarsdale, New York: Bradbury Press, 1974. ISBN 0-02-776190-8.
A circus of shapes parade throughout this easy-to-read book.

Ross, Anna. *Little Grover's Book of Shapes.* Illustrated by Norman Gorbaty. New York: Random House, 1992. ISBN 0-679-82237-2.
Little Grover discovers all the shapes around him.

Scarry, Richard. *Lowly Worm's Shapes and Sizes.* New York: Simon and Schuster, 1998. ISBN 0-689-81654-5.
Lowly Worm bends and shows shapes with a little help from his Busytown friends.

Scarry, Richard. *Shapes and Opposites.* New York: J. B. Communications, Inc., 1995. ISBN 1-56144-724-2.
The loveable characters of Richard Scarry's Busytown tell all about shapes and opposites.

Seah, Jeffrey. *Shapes.* Illustrated by Alain Fontaine. Singapore: Mighty Minds Corporation, 1994. ISBN 0-981-3053-71-2.
Likeable characters and colorful illustrations introduce shapes.

Shapes. Photographs by George Siede and Donna Preis. Lincolnwood, Illinois: Publications International Ltd., 1992. ISBN 1-56173-481-0.
Color photographs of familiar objects show basic shapes.

Shapes. Photographs by George Siede and Donna Preis. 2nd edition. Lincolnwood, Illinois: Publications International Ltd., 1995. ISBN 0-7853-1283-8.
Ordinary objects appear in a variety of shapes.

Thomas The Tank Engine Shapes and Sizes. Illustrated by Deborah Colvin Borgo. New York: Random House, 1991. ISBN 0-679-81643-7.
Thomas introduces basic sizes and shapes in this small board book.

Tiny Toon Adventures First Book of Shapes. New York: Heinemann, 1992. ISBN 0-434-96044-6.
The Tiny Toon characters introduce a variety of shapes as they play.

Turner, Gwenda. *Shapes.* New York: Viking Kestrel, 1991. ISBN 0-670-83744-X.
Children learn all about shapes in this clever cutout book.

Vischer, Phil. *Pa Grape's Shapes.* Nashville, Tennessee: Tommy Nelson, Inc., 1997. ISBN 0-8499-1507-4.
Pa Grape has to use a tire machine to make the perfect shape for tires for his car.

White, Stephen. *Baby Bop Discovers Shapes.* Illustrated by Larry Daste. Allen, Texas: The Lyons Group, 1993. ISBN 1-57064-010-6.
Baby Bop invites the reader to help her find shapes.

Worth, Bonnie. *Muppet Babies Shape Machine.* Illustrated by Kathy Spahr. Chicago: Childrens Press, 1988. ISBN 0-516-09075-5.
The Muppet Babies find a machine that makes all sorts of shapes.

Colors and Shapes

Groening, Matt, and Maggie Groening. *Maggie Simpson's Book of Colors and Shapes.* Illustrated by Matt Groening. New York: HarperCollins, 1991.

The Simpson family uses familiar objects to introduce colors and shapes.

Hill, Eric. *Spot's Big Book of Colors, Shapes, and*

Numbers. New York: G. P. Putnam's Sons, 1994. ISBN 0-399-22679-6.

Spot and his friends have fun with colors, shapes, and numbers.

Hillert, Margaret. *I Like Things*. Illustrated by Lois Axeman. Cleveland, Ohio: Modern Curriculum Press, 1982. ISBN 0-8136-5102-6; 0-8136-5602-8 (pbk).

Children categorize things by color, size, and shape.

Reed, Giles. *Learn Shapes and Colors with the Munch Bunch*. Windermere, Florida: Rourke Publications, 1981. ISBN 0-86625-0794.

The activities of the Munch Bunch provide practice in recognizing colors and shapes.

Thompson, Emily. *Big Bird's Square Meal: Stories about Shapes and Colors*. Illustrated by Tom Brannon. New York: Golden Press, 1988. ISBN 0-307-13107-6.

Big Bird, Elmo, and Cookie Monster go on a picnic, where they see many shapes, while Bert introduces Ernie to the world of colors.

COLORS AND SHAPES ACTIVITIES

Read some of the beginner books that feature photographs of familiar objects to the class. Divide the class into some groups to create a photographic essay about colors or shapes. Each group must choose a theme, then collect objects that can be grouped together either by color or shape, take photographs of the objects, and use the photos to make a photo essay. The photos can be used on a poster, book, or even a bulletin board.

After sharing *Big Bird's Red Book,* by Rosanne and Jonathan Cerf, have the class brainstorm a list of more red things. Have the class (in small groups or as one large group) write another color adventure for Big Bird or another of the *Sesame Street* characters. Choose one color and brainstorm a list of things found in that color.

Have a "Great Colors" contest. Assign each child to write two or more sentences describing their favorite color.

Divide the class into small groups of two or three. Have the group choose a theme and a color to use to create a color book. Brainstorm a list of ordinary things that can be found in the selected color. Use the list as a basis to create a board book using pictures and drawings of the objects.

Read *Disney's Pocahontas, Painting with the Wind: A Book about Color,* by Teddy Slater, and Bobbie Kalman's *Colors of Nature.* Discuss colors and nature. Choose some facet of nature and write a brief poem or paragraph describing the colors associated with it. Some examples might include the lush green of a summer forest, the deep blue of an ocean wave, or the black clouds of a threatening thunderstorm.

Make a color scrapbook. Cut out or draw pictures of things found in different colors. Glue each color group on separate sheets of white paper. Label the color at the top of the page. Punch holes on the pages and use yarn to tie the pages together in the color scrapbook.

REFERENCES

Beard, Ruth. *An Outline of Piaget's Developmental Psychology for Students and Teachers*. New York: Basic Books, 1969.

Benyon, Laurie. "Art: Shapes—Color Zoo." *School Library Media Activities Monthly* (February 1996): 15–16.

Bittinger, Gayle. *1–2–3 Shapes: Beginning Shape Activities for Young Children*. Everett, Washington: Warren Publishing House, Inc., 1994.

Brodie, Carolyn. "A Moveable Feast; Pop-Ups, Fold-Outs, and Pull Tabs."*School Library Journal* (September 1989): 162–167.

Butler, Dorothy. *Babies Need Books*. New York: Atheneum, 1980.

Carlson, Ann D. "Letters, Numbers, Shapes and Colors: Getting a Grasp on Concept Books." *School Library Journal* (May 1995): 30–33.

Clancy, Jeanne Marie. "Board Books Come of Age." *School Library Journal* (July 1989): 34–35.

"Colors." *Kidstuff*. 7: 3.

Cullinan, Bernice E., Mary K. Karner, and Arlene M. Pillar. *Literature and the Child*. San Diego, California: Harcourt Brace Jovanovich, 1991.

DeSalvo, Nancy. *Beginning with Books: Library Programming for Infants, Toddlers, and Preschoolers*. Hamden, Connecticut: Library Professional Publicatons, 1993.

Elleman, Barbara. "Colors." *BookLinks* (July 1992): 31–34.

Elleman, Barbara. "Illustrations As Art: Color." *BookLinks* (May 1995): 58–61.

Elleman, Barbara. "Illustrations As Art: Shape." *BookLinks* (March 1996): 52–55.

Evans, Dilys. "Literacy through Art." *BookLinks* (15 December 1990): 832–37.

Greenberg, Jan. "The Shapes and Colors of Modern Art." *BookLinks* (May 1992): 34–38.

Hanley, Karen Stang. "Board Books." *BookLinks* (July 1995): 43–47.

Huck, Charlotte S., Susan Hepler, and Janet Hickman. *Children's Literature in the Elementary School*. 5th ed. Fort Worth, Texas: Harcourt, Brace College Publishers, 1993.

Hurst, Carol Otis. "Rainbow Reading." *Teaching K–8* (March 1991): 81–82.

Kladder, Jeri. *Story Hour: 55 Preschool Programs for Public Libraries*. Jefferson, North Carolina: McFarland & Company, Inc., 1995.

Laughlin, Mildren Knight, and Terri Parker Street. *Literature-Based Art and Music: Children's Books and Activities to Enrich the K–5 Curriculum*. Phoenix, Arizona: Oryx Press, 1992.

MacDonald, Margaret Read. *Booksharing: 101 Programs to Use with Preschoolers*. Hamden, Connecticut: Library Professional Publications, 1988.

McElmeel, Sharron L. *McElmeel's Booknotes: Literature across the Curriculum*. Englewood, Colorado: Teacher Ideas Press, 1993.

May, Lola. "Shapes Are Everywhere." *Teaching K–8* (March 1994): 26–27.

Meyerhoff, Michael K, and Burton L. White. "Making the Grade As Parents." *Psychology Today* (September 1986): 38–45.

Paulin, Mary Ann. *Creative Uses of Children's Literature*. Hamden, Connecticut: Library Professional Publications, 1982.

"Rhyme's Reason." *Working Mother* (October 1996): 82.

Russell, Cheryl. Color. Huntington Beach, California: Teacher Created Materials, Inc., 1993.

"Simply Shapes." *Kidstuff* 6: 9.

Sobut, Mary A., and Bonnie Neuman Bogen. *Whole Language Literature Activities for Young Children*. West Nyack, New York: The Center for Applied Research in Education, 1993.

Sutherland, Zena, and May Hill Arbuthnot. *Children and Books*. 8th edition. New York: HarperCollins Publishers, 1991.

Taylor, Barbara. *Over the Rainbow: The Science of Color and Light*. New York: Random House, 1992.

Trotter, Robert J. "You've Come a Long Way, Baby." *Psychology Today* (May 1987): 34–35.

Warren, Jean. *1-2-3 Colors: Color Day Activities for Young Children*. Everett, Washington: Warren Publishing House, 1988.

Webster's New World Dictionary of the American Language. 2nd college edition. New York: The World Publishing Company, 1970.

White, Burton L., Tiffany Field, Andrew N. Meltzoff, and Jerome Kagan. "Baby Research Comes of Age." *Psychology Today* (May 1987): 46–47.

INDEX

ABOUT THE AUTHOR

Cathie Hilterbran Cooper (B.S., Ohio University; M.L.S., Kent State University) is the district media coordinator for Adena Local School District in Frankfort, Ohio. She has been a library/media specialist for twenty-three years at both high school and primary levels. For the past six years, she added district technology coordinator to those duties. In addition, she has worked as a branch director and children's and reference librarian in a public library. She has published several articles in professional journals. Her first book was *The Storyteller's Cornucopia* (Alleyside Press 1992, 1998), followed by *ABC Books and Activities: From Preschool to High School* (Scarecrow Press, Inc. 1996) and *Counting Your Way through 1-2-3 Books and Activities* (Scarecrow Press, Inc. 1997). She resides in Grove City, Ohio, with her husband and two children.